'I love the realism and d [...] book. It is truly an example [...] road". Emily has learned h [...] times and what she shares f [...] .....experiences is very inspiring.'

Marilyn Baker,
singer/songwriter and Director, MBM Trust

'*The Power of Seven* in seven words: personal, biblical, moving, challenging, compassionate, inspiring and powerful. Yet seven words are not enough to describe this beautiful devotional. Written from Emily Owen's passionate heart, it stirred my own. *The Power of Seven* reminded me of who I am in Christ, and more importantly, who Christ is in me.'

Catherine Campbell, author

'Whenever I recall meeting and teaching alongside Emily Owen, I can only say, "Thank you, God, for this precious woman!" Emily has a powerful message of overcoming great obstacles, lives a daily life of joyful devotion to our Lord and exudes a passion for God's Word and for passing on its truths to others. Her books – and her heart – point us to God, lift up our Saviour, and strengthen our faith and trust in him.'

Elizabeth George, author

'Emily invites us into a profound and personal conversation with God, helping us to see him in the minutiae of domestic family life, the pressure of daily life and in our darkest moments. She allows us to briefly inhabit her inner world of silence and love, giving voice to our deepest needs with humanity and humour, and sometimes with the poetic sparseness and simplicity of a haiku. This is a gem of a book that reminds us of our deep need for relationship with our Creator, and helps us to know, lean into and rest in the Lord.'

Kate Nicholas, preacher,
Christian broadcaster and author

'The conversational style of Emily's stories and the lyrical character of God's word to us make for a lovely combination. The insights about God's purposes for us are very deep and enriching and I shall want to return to this.'

Reverend Canon Chris Oxley

'If you have ever wondered what it means to be in conversation with God then this book is for you. The combination of Bible reflection, personal stories and the beautifully expressed conversations with God drew me right into his heart and filled me with joy. This book will certainly be my journey's companion in the weeks to come.'

Tracy Williamson,
author and speaker with MBM Trust

'Emily's heart for God and resilience in life shines through her writing. She writes powerfully and creatively, capturing the heartbeat of God in every sentence.'

Tania Harris,
pastor, speaker and founder of GodConversations.com

THE POWER
OF SEVEN

49 devotional reflections
7 biblical themes
Genesis to Revelation

Emily Owen

Authentic

First published 2018 by Authentic Media Limited,
PO Box 6326, Bletchley, Milton Keynes, MK1 9GG.
authenticmedia.co.uk

British Library Cataloguing in Publication Data
A catalogue record for this book is available from the British Library.
ISBN: 978-1-78078-990-3
978-1-78078-991-0 (e-book)

Cover design by Margarita Dimova
facebook.com/DeSignStudio.iMAGlingarCh

Printed and bound by CPI Group (UK) Ltd, Croydon, CR0 4YY

Contents

Acknowledgements   viii
Preface   ix

Part 1   **Creation**   **3**
   1   Light   5
   2   Sky   8
   3   Land, Plants and Trees   12
   4   Sun, Moon and Stars   16
   5   Fish and Birds   20
   6   Animals and People   24
   7   Rest   28

Part 2   **God *Is***   **31**
   8   God *Is* My Rock   33
   9   God *Is* My Fortress   37
   10   God *Is* My Deliverer   41
   11   God *Is* My Refuge   44
   12   God *Is* My Shield   48
   13   God *Is* My Salvation   52
   14   God *Is* My Stronghold   55

Part 3	**The Lord Is My Shepherd**	**59**
15	He Lets Me Rest in Green Meadows	61
16	He Leads Me beside Peaceful Streams	66
17	He Renews My Strength	70
18	He Guides Me along Right Paths	74
19	Your Rod and Your Staff Protect and Comfort Me	78
20	You Prepare a Feast for Me in the Presence of My Enemies	82
21	You Honour Me by Anointing My Head with Oil	86
Part 4	**I AM**	**91**
22	I AM the Light of the World	93
23	I AM the Way, the Truth and the Life	96
24	I AM the Door	99
25	I AM the Good Shepherd	103
26	I AM the Vine	107
27	I AM the Bread of Life	111
28	I AM the Resurrection and the Life	116
Part 5	**Echoes from the Cross**	**121**
29	Father, Forgive	123
30	Today You Will Be with Me in Paradise	126
31	Woman, Here Is Your Son	130
32	My God, My God, Why Have You Forsaken Me?	134

33	I Thirst!	138
34	It Is Finished	142
35	Into Your Hands I Commit My Spirit	146
Part 6	**Add to Faith**	**151**
36	Goodness	153
37	Knowledge	157
38	Self-control	160
39	Perseverance	163
40	Godliness	166
41	Mutual Affection	170
42	Love	173
Part 7	**Revelation Churches**	**177**
43	Ephesus	181
44	Smyrna	184
45	Pergamum	187
46	Thyatira	190
47	Sardis	193
48	Philadelphia	196
49	Laodicea	199
	Notes	205

You can read more about Emily and her books at:
www.emily-owen.com
facebook.com/EmilyOwenAuthor
or
twitter.com/EmilyOwenAuthor

Preface

I was young when I learned that there are number patterns in the Bible. I don't remember them all but I do remember that 'seven' is biblically significant.

For those who picked up this book hoping to find a book about formulae and algorithms and other mathematical complexities, I'm afraid you'll be disappointed. Despite having mathematicians in my family, ability with numbers passed me by. More than passed me by; it never even came close.

This book looks at the number seven in a non-mathematical way. It doesn't ask why there are groups of seven in the Bible, it asks what they can teach us.

Taking each part of each seven individually, and in a meditational/devotional style, the book includes personal anecdotes,[1] stories, reflections and prayers.

Creation
God *Is*
The Lord Is My Shepherd

I AM
Echoes from the Cross
Add to Faith
Revelation Churches

Seven lots of seven = seven weeks (if I got the sum correct!), so that's forty-nine days during which, I pray, you'll be gently challenged, encouraged, and affirmed in your relationship with God.

Ephesians 3:16,17: 'I pray that out of his glorious riches he may strengthen you with power through his Spirit in your inner being, so that Christ may dwell in your hearts through faith.'

Philippians 1:6: 'And I am certain that God, who began the good work within you, will continue his work until it is finally finished on the day when Christ Jesus returns' (NLT).

Thank you to every person who has ever shown me what it means to walk with God.
The God who made the stars.
The God who holds all things together.
The God who knows me better than I know myself.
Without him, I would not be.

Emily

For Teresa

Remember how you despaired of my ineptitude with
anything scientific or mathematical?
You'd have been amused to see a book of mine with
'seven' in the title.
But you won't see it.
Because you're seeing far, far better things.
As you said, you're 'partying in heaven before me'.
Don't forget to save me a quiet corner.

God has wiped every tear from your eyes, and there is no
more death or sorrow or crying or pain.
(See Rev. 21:4.)

Genesis 1:2: 'Now the earth was formless and empty, darkness was over the surface of the deep, and the Spirit of God was hovering over the waters.'

Part 1

Creation

The paper was blank.
My niece picked up a pen.
'I'm going to draw a house.'
A few seconds later, she handed the pen to me;
'Can you draw me a house?'
She couldn't do it.
Artist I am not, but I managed to produce something vaguely resembling a house.
The paper wasn't blank any more.
She'd asked me to fill it,
and I did.

'In the beginning, God . . .'
The Bible starts with these words.
God there,
in the beginning,
before anything.
But what happened after the beginning?
After the time when there was God

and nothing else?
Well, God spoke.
He said,
'Let there be . . .'
and, out of nothing,
came something.
'Let there be . . .'

With God, nothing becomes something.
Always.
Out of the nothing times,
the hard times,
the lonely times,
the busy times,
the unknowing times,
come something times.
He speaks into the darkness,
as no one else can:
'Let there be . . .'
And there is.

2 Corinthians 4:6: 'For God, who said, 'Let there be light
in the darkness,' has made this light shine in our hearts so
we could know the glory of God that is seen in the face of
Jesus Christ' (NLT).

Light

The LORD is my light and my salvation – whom shall I fear?
Psalm 27:1

I was camping with my sister. One night, we crawled into our little tent and settled in our sleeping bags. Lying side by side, we whispered to each other before eventually drifting off to sleep. But we didn't sleep for long. We were both suddenly woken by something.

Or lack of something.

As we peered through the gloom around us, we realized we could see the other tents on the field, but we couldn't see our own.
Our tent had blown away.

We lay there, looking around us in confusion, until one of us – I can't remember which – looked up.
Nudging the other, she whispered 'look' as she pointed upwards.
The other tents were not the only thing we could see.
We could also see the stars.

When the tent was over us, the stars were there but obscured.
Take the tent away, though, and we could see them.
We could see the stars.

Perhaps we sometimes try to look at God 'through a tent'.
Try and see him through all the other stuff we have going
on in our lives.
Wondering where he is as we obscure him.

Why are you blocking me out?
Why are you letting 'stuff' prevent you from seeing me?
Why don't you want my light?

My sister and I had a choice;
worry about the tent – or stuff – or look at the stars.
The stars were beautiful.

Father God
Thank you that you created light.
I'm sorry that I create things which block you and your
light out.
I do want your light.
I need it.
Help me to let my tents blow away,
and to look at the stars.
I'm so glad you're there.
Amen.

Why did I create light?
I created light because I want you to see.

To see what I can do.
To see what I am offering you.
To see to live.
That's why I said, 'Let there be light.'

Let there be light instead of darkness.
Hope, not despair.
I offer that hope to you.
Here is light – please take it.

Let there be light instead of darkness.
Joy, not dread.
I offer that joy to you.
Here is light – please take it.

Let there be light instead of darkness.
Peace, not fear.
I offer that peace to you.
Here is light – please take it.

Let there be light instead of darkness.
Security, not doubt.
I offer that security to you.
Here is light – please take it.

I said, 'Let there be light.'
And there was.
There is.
There really is.
And it is good.

2

Sky

Your love, LORD, reaches to the heavens, your faithfulness to the skies.

Psalm 36:5

Near where I grew up is a museum. Referred to by us as 'the dinosaur museum', it has a life-size model of a dinosaur skeleton in one of its rooms.

When my sister was 2 years old, we took her to the dinosaur museum. We told her all about the dinosaur and how exciting it was to see. When we arrived, we rushed straight to the dinosaur room and watched for her reaction.

Nothing.

She looked around, again and again, bewildered.
Eventually, my dad crouched down next to her and asked what was wrong.
'There's no dinosaur,' she sobbed.

Dad, still squatting beside her, looked around,
and realized.
She was stuck on her level.

She wasn't looking up.
There was a huge dinosaur skeleton towering over her, but she missed it.
Because she didn't look up.

Dad lifted her head . . . and she saw it.
She saw the dinosaur.
And her little hands automatically reached up towards it in amazement.

God, in Jesus, came to us.
Comes to us.
He shares our problems.
He understands our disappointments.
He understands our confusion.
He crouches down to our level.
He gently lifts our heads.
And he points us to God.
Do you see?
Are you amazed?

Lord God
Thank you that I can never sink so low that
you won't crouch down beside me.
And gently lift me up.
Lifting my head.
Encouraging me to see you.
Help me not to resist,
but to reach for all you offer me.
Amen.

Why did I create sky?
I created sky because I want you to reach.
To reach for what I am offering you.
To reach for me.
And let me tell you what you can reach for . . .

You can reach for patience.
When you're at the end of your tether
and the world is driving you mad.
Reach up.
I'm here.

You can reach for comfort.
When things seem out of control
and you're all jangled inside.
Reach up.
I'm here.

You can reach for guidance.
When you're at a crossroads and there are
so many paths you could choose.
Which is the right one?
The wrong one?
The dead end?
Reach up.
I'm here.

Yes, there will be clouds in the sky.
They won't be there forever,
but they will come.

We can deal with them.
Together.
But it's up to you.
If you reach up,
I'm here.

3

Land, Plants and Trees

The joy of the LORD is your strength.

Nehemiah 8:10

I was in a wheelchair the time we passed an arrow pointing in the direction of a waterfall, indicating a path which led through a forest. Probably not good for wheelchairs, so I told the others that they should go on and I would wait for them. But, knowing I love waterfalls, they rejected that plan and said that they would get me there.

At first, the going was good. Apart from people heading away from the waterfall giving us strange looks, we were fine. As we continued, the path got narrower and the strange looks intensified. But we pressed on anyway. Eventually, the path disappeared altogether, along with our confusion about the strange looks. This was clearly not a wheelchair-friendly route to take.

Again, I told my family to leave me behind, but they wouldn't. Instead, they pushed and pulled and shoved me and my chair along. Towards the end, as we neared the waterfall, the 'path' was so non-existent that they had to literally carry me over rocks and tree roots.

But eventually we got to the top.
We reached the waterfall.
We made it.
Together.
The journey up that mountain was tough.
It was a struggle for all of us.
But it was also a journey full of laughter.
As we negotiated obstacle after obstacle,
we did so together,
encouraging each other,
enjoying each other's company.
We had chosen to stick together, so that's what we did.
And, when we made it to the top,
we enjoyed the waterfall together, too.

Sometimes life is good.
Sometimes it is a struggle.
But we don't need to do it on our own.
God will never go on ahead without us.
He stays.
Negotiating the twists and turns,
the ups and downs,
the highs and lows.
Carrying us when we need it.
And enjoying the view from the top with us.
Every time we make it to the waterfall.
Together.

Lord God
Thank you that we're in this journey together.
You won't leave me behind.
Thank you for carrying me when I can't go on.
It's so good to share the ups
and the downs
with you.
And to enjoy the view from the top when we get there.
Together.
Amen.

Why did I create land? And plants? And trees?
I created them because I want you to enjoy.
I made the world for you – so enjoy it!
Let me tell you about it . . .

I made the land, the plains and the mountains,
so that you will always have a firm place to stand.
It may be a high place,
it may be a low place, but
walk it with me and it will always
be a safe place.
So, step out in the knowledge of my presence.
And enjoy.

I made the plants, every single flower, to add colour to your
life.
To add variety.
To give you pleasure.
You're so busy, dashing here and there.

Slow down.
Take a moment.
Enjoy the flowers around you.
Bury your nose in their scent.
Drink in their beauty.
Arrange them in a vase.
Make a daisy chain.
Take pleasure in the flowers.
I made them for you.
Slow down.
And enjoy.

I made the trees to show you my protection.
They give you shade from the heat,
shelter from the storm,
a refuge from the wind.
And they can do all that because they are rooted.
They put their roots deep into the ground and they hold on tight.
I can protect you from the storms that come your way.
You don't have to do it alone.
Root yourself deep in me.
And hold on tight.

I want you to take pleasure from life,
whatever shape it takes.
I made all this for you.
Enjoy!

4

Sun, Moon and Stars

For God is working in you, giving you the desire and the power to do what pleases him.

Philippians 2:13 (NLT)

In 2012, the Olympics and Paralympics were held in London, and the news was full of sport. One picture showed a blind runner crossing the finishing line. His guide was right next to him, the two men being attached at the wrist so that the blind athlete would know which direction to run in.

The guide kept pace with the athlete during the race, never going off and leaving him, offering encouragement and direction throughout. In fact, the two worked so closely together that, despite only one being a para athlete, they were considered a team.

They finished the race together.

They both received medals.

As might be expected, most media attention was on the blind runner.

But what was the first thing he did when interviewed?

He thanked his guide.
He recognized his teammate.

We have a guide as we go through life.
God is with us every step of the way.
Helping, encouraging, enabling,
never going off and leaving us.
But people out there will focus on us,
unless we thank our guide.
Unless we recognize our teammate.
Unless we give God the worship and the glory
he deserves.
Don't forget!

Lord God
When I look at my life, I often feel as though I am running
in the dark.
I'm not sure where I am going.
Or which way to turn.
I need a guide.
Thank you that you step in and run alongside me,
showing me the way.
You're always there.
But sometimes I forget.
I take you for granted.
Help me remember to acknowledge you.
Glorify you.
Worship you.
Amen.

Why did I create the sun, moon and stars?
I created them because
I want you to worship.
I want you to look up at the majesty in the sky and say,
wow –
my God made that.

I made the sun to remind you to worship me on good days.
Days when all is going well.
Days full of laughter.
Your favourite days.
Worship me in the good times –
don't let them make you forget
I'm here.

I made the moon to remind you to worship me in bad times.
When you're stuck in the night
and it seems day will never come.
Times when you don't even want day to come.
Find the moonlight.
Find me.
And stick with me.
I'm still your God.
Worship me in the bad times –
don't let them make you forget
I'm here.

I made the stars to remind you to worship me during in-
between times.
When it's not light and not dark.

When life is just ticking along.
Nothing changes.
Same old routine.
And then you see a star.
You see a God moment.
And it takes your breath away.
Look for the stars,
every day.
You'll find them.
I know you will,
because I put them there.
Worship me in the in-between times –
don't let them make you forget
I'm here.

I'm here.
Worship me.

5

Fish and Birds

It is for freedom that Christ has set us free. Stand firm, then, and do not let yourselves be burdened again by a yoke of slavery.

Galatians 5:1

Our new dog ran off. He didn't come back. We called and called his name, but he paid no attention. Eventually, another dog owner managed to catch him and bring him back to us. As we re-clipped his lead on, we realized: Jasper hadn't yet learned his name. In the rescue kennels, they had called him Coke, but we decided Jasper suited him better, so we gave him a new name.

The thing was, it took Jasper time to get the hang of it.
A while to learn who he was and who he now belonged to.
When we let Jasper off the lead that day, he certainly had freedom.
But he had too much of it.
He had no security within his freedom,
no boundaries.
And he just ended up running around in circles.

A week or so later, we let him off again, and the difference was clear. He knew his name, knew who he was with and so, rather than dashing aimlessly all over the place, he was able to relax and enjoy being a dog. He made sure he was aware of where we were, came back to us from time to time, and enjoyed finding new smells and playing with other dogs.

And he knew his name.

Isaiah 62:2,3: 'you will be given a new name by the LORD's own mouth. The LORD will hold you in his hand for all to see – a splendid crown in the hand of God' (NLT).

When you turn to God, he gives you a new name.

He gives you a sense of belonging.

He gives you a new type of freedom.

Freedom within the security of Someone who does not want you to get lost.

Who does not want you to dash around aimlessly,

becoming more and more tired,

weighed down within your own idea of freedom.

Freedom in Someone who knows your name.

Lord God

Thank you that you know my name.

Sometimes I don't know it myself.

I forget who I am and

Who I belong to.

Help me to relax in the knowledge

that you have set me free.

I am known by you.

Amen.

Why did I create the fish and the birds?
I created them because I want you to be free.
Free to soar with me.
Free to swim with me.
Let me tell you what I mean . . .

Look at the birds.
They fly so high!
Sometimes they flap their wings.
Sometimes they don't even do that.
They just ride the wind.
They simply be.
Not doing,
just being.
Just being,
not worrying.
Not missing the moment,
wondering whether the wind will support them.
They just let the wind do its job.

What about you?
Do you let me do my job?
I will support you.
I promise I won't let you fall.
So just be.
Be free.
In me.

Look at the fish.
They swim in oceans, rivers, streams, ponds, tanks . . .

If there's water, fish will swim.
It's what they love.
It's what they live for.
It's what they were made to do.
And that doesn't change,
even when the water does.
Sometimes the water is clean.
Sometimes it's dirty.
Sometimes the water is shallow.
Sometimes it's deep.
Sometimes the water is full of friends.
Sometimes the reverse is true.
Whatever the situation,
fish will swim.

What about you?
Whatever your situation,
will you be free?
You can be.
In me.
I promise.
I'll help you.
I made you for freedom.
So let go and
be free.

6

Animals and People

. . . teach me your ways so I may know you . . .

Exodus 33:13

I can remember the day as if it were yesterday. We had been waiting for it for months. The arrival of my sister's first baby. I remember the mad dash to the hospital, finding a car parking space, heading up to the maternity ward, looking around for my sister, then hurrying over and getting my first glimpse of my niece. We passed baby Abigail round carefully, being sure that each of us had lots of cuddle time. She was perfect.

At one point, her father, my brother-in-law, was holding her. He looked down at his sleeping baby, and said in awe; 'Wow. My life will never be the same again.'
He's not alone.
Nearly everyone who has a child finds their life has been turned upside down! Someone new has entered their life. It's not all about 'me' any more.
There's someone else to think about, to get to know, to consider, to put first.

A bit like when we meet God.
Life will never be the same again.
Or at least it shouldn't be.
But do you find yourself slipping back?
Back into putting yourself first?
Putting you before God?
Or do you remember that God is there for you
to know better?
He's waiting to be involved in every day.
Life will never be the same again.
And that's good.

Psalm 16:11: 'You make known to me the path of life; you will fill me with joy in your presence, with eternal pleasures at your right hand.'

Lord God
Thank you for coming into my life.
And thank you for wanting to.
Help me to know you better every day.
To always put you first.
It's not all about me any more.
Amen.

Why did I create animals and people?
Or, to be more specific, why did I create you?
I created you because
I want you to know.
To know I made you.
To know you are wanted.

To know you are mine.
I didn't have to make you.
I did so with purpose.
Let me tell you about it . . .

Before I created you, I looked around at the world I'd made.
I saw that it was good.
For a while, that was fine,
but I knew there was something missing.
And that something was you.

Majestic though the stars and trees and oceans are,
they can't relate to me.
They can't sit down and have a chat with me.
They can't get to know me.
But you can.
And that's why I made you.
Because I want you to know . . .
Me.

It's not difficult.
I'm not a million miles away.
I'm right here.
I'm here when you wake up.
And I'm still here when you go to sleep.
I've not left you.

I was there when you went to work.
I was there when you had lunch with a friend.
I was there when you picked your children up from school.

Did you see me?
Did you remember?
Did you know I was there?

Whatever your day brings, never doubt me.
Why would I go anywhere?
I love you!
I want to spend time with you,
and do you know why?
Because
of
you.

I know you.
Do you know me?

7

Rest

Then God blessed the seventh day and made it holy, because on it he rested from all the work of creating that he had done.

Genesis 2:3

The house I grew up in had a lovely couple living next door. They seemed incredibly old to me, and always assured my mum that they 'never heard the noise' when she apologized for the loud voices and giggles that would regularly float over the fence from her four girls. The couple even allowed us to play in their garden – their lawn was much better for badminton and tennis.

One summer, things had been quite difficult for our family, and there was a knock on the door.

Our neighbours:

'You need a break. Why don't you go and spend a couple of weeks in our caravan by the sea? It is so peaceful, and a place to get away from everything for a bit.'

God is closer than a next-door neighbour.

And he is also someone who says, 'You need a break.'

Whether things are going well or not.

I know you need a rest.
I made you, remember?
And, what's more, I know what it is like to take a break.
So I know how beneficial, how essential it is.
Which is why I want it for you.
You are important enough for me to set you an example;
am I important enough for you to follow it?

Lord God
Resting is hard.
I am so bad at it.
I just think I need to keep going.
But you're right, of course.
I do need to stop sometimes.
Thank you for setting me an example.
You are important enough for me to follow it.
Amen.

Why didn't I make anything today?
Why did I take a break?
I took a break because I want you to rest.
I want you to know that it's OK to take time out.
It is more than OK.

When you're so busy that your feet hardly touch the ground . . .
Rest.
Breathe.
It's OK to take time out.

When you're pulled in all directions and feel as though you
will snap . . .
Rest.
Breathe.
It's OK to take time out.

When your 'to-do' list is growing, deadlines are looming,
pressure is building . . .
Rest.
Breathe.
It's OK to take time out.

When I made you, I made a person, not a machine.
No one expects you to keep going 24/7 –
least of all me.

So, my child,
be sure to make time to do
one of the things I created you to do:
Rest.
I chose rest, too.
It's more than OK.

Part 2

God *Is*

Psalm 18:2: 'The LORD is my rock, my fortress and my deliverer; my God is my rock, in whom I take refuge, my shield and the horn of my salvation, my stronghold.'

In order to appreciate what is being said, sometimes it can be helpful to look at what is not being said.
So, when we read Psalm 18:2, what we don't see is 'was'.
Or 'might be'.
Or 'will think about being'.
No, we see 'is'.

Rock. Fortress. Deliverer. Refuge. Shield. Salvation. Stronghold.

The Lord our God is those Psalm 18:2 things.
For each one of us.
For you.

'Is' means 'to be present'.
Here.

Right now.
God *Is* . . .

Psalm 46:1: 'God is our refuge and strength, an ever-present help in trouble.'

8

God *Is* My Rock

Cast your cares on the LORD and he will sustain you . . .

Psalm 55:22

I was terrified. Two days before, I'd had brain surgery, which had caused me to lose all my hearing. Silence was scary and then, due to the horrendous headaches I was experiencing, I was told I needed a lumbar puncture. A procedure to take some fluid from my spine, via injection. Which meant I'd need to move from lying flat on my back and bend over, giving access to my spine. I was very weak from the surgery and so, while I could possibly manage to sit on the edge of my bed and lean forward, I knew I wouldn't be able to hold the position for very long.

This logistical problem caused a bit of discussion. What would we do? The doctors didn't know. I certainly didn't know.

Then my dad stepped forward.

He knelt on the floor beside my bed. When I leaned forward, he was there. Supporting me. I didn't nosedive;

I rested against him. The floor was hard. It probably hurt Dad's knees. Especially when he was also bearing my weight. Yet he didn't move.

With an action more eloquent than words, he shared in what I was going through.
More than that, he enabled me to get through it.
I couldn't have done it without him.

We have a God who steps into our situations.

When we are weak and can't go on: He's there.

Lean on me.

When we are out of options: He's there.

Lean on me.

When we try to manage on our own but can't: He's there.

Lean on me.

When we don't know what to do: He's there.

Lean on me.

When we are in a place we'd never choose: He's there.

Lean on me.

He's there.
Full stop.

Lean on me.

Father God
Sometimes, I can't do it.
I want to, but I can't.
And often I forget that I don't need to.
I just need to lean on you.
Thank you for being there.
Thank you for supporting me.
Help me remember to lean on you.
Amen.

You have a Rock.
Me.
Do you know what that means?
It means I'm going nowhere.
You can push me away all you like,
but you won't move me.
I won't budge.
I don't want to.
You have a Rock.
Me.
Which means I'm going nowhere.
When you're tired,
or unsure,
or scared,
lean on me.

I won't budge.
But I will support you.
Rest on me.
Let me be your strength.
You have a Rock.
Me.
My child; do you know what that means?
You have a Rock.

9

God *Is* My Fortress

If you look for me wholeheartedly, you will find me.
Jeremiah 29:13 (NLT)

The doorbell rang and, as he left the house, my dad answered it. When I was growing up, the doorbell rang frequently. Neighbours calling round. Friends dropping in. Parents bringing their children for my mum, a childminder, to take care of. Dad opened the door and saw a mum with a baby on her hip. Hardly looking at them as he rushed by, he said, 'In you go, she's in the kitchen.'

When he returned, the mum and baby were still there. This time, he looked at them properly. He didn't recognize the child, but there was something familiar about the baby's mum. It was his sister-in-law, flown all the way from Australia. He'd not expected her, so he'd missed her.

Dad had not been surprised to see a mum and child at the door, so that's what he'd seen.
And that's why he'd stopped looking.
He'd seen the situation, but he'd missed who was in the situation.

How often we do the same with God.

We look at our situation and then, in trying to deal with it, we stop looking.
And we miss who is in our situations.
All of them.
We stop looking.
And we miss God.
In our not looking, we overlook his presence.
We miss it.
We overlook our God who says, 'I'm here.'

I'm right here.
Don't stop looking.

When you look for him, you'll find him.
When you find him, you'll know him.
When you know him, he won't be missing.

Where's God in this?
Why not have a look . . .

Father God
It's awful to think I miss you.
You're right there
all around
and yet I miss you.
I get so wrapped up in my situation
that I forget it's not my situation.
It's our situation.

We're in it together.
Help me to look for you,
find you,
know you.
Amen.

You have a Fortress.
Me.
Do you know what that means?
It means I'm here.
Every way you look.
Right, left, forwards, backwards . . .
any way you look,
I'm here.
Surrounding you.
You know those situations you face?
Those doubts?
Those challenges?
Those scary times?
Let me tell you something:
I'm closer than them.
So, any time you look at anything,
face anything,
live anything,
I'm there too.
You're looking at me.
Or at least, you can be.
Don't look through me.
Look for me.
I'm not hiding.

You'll find me.
Because you have a Fortress.
Me.
My child; do you know what that means?
You have a Fortress.

10

God *Is* My Deliverer

Your own ears will hear him. Right behind you a voice will say,
'This is the way you should go,' whether to the right or to the left.
Isaiah 30:21 (NLT)

The boy runs on ahead. He has spotted a tree which looks perfect for climbing. Impatient with the slow pace of his family, he speeds on. Maybe he'll be able to climb quickly and hide. He giggles to himself as he imagines his mum and dad looking for him while he watches them from his treetop perch. The tree is quite easy to climb and soon he is near the top. He pauses and looks down. His parents are beginning to look for him. Stifling a laugh, he quietly climbs higher in the tree. Once at the top, he looks down again. This time he does not laugh. He can tell, by the way his mum is running her hands through her hair, she is worried. She can't find him and it's not funny any more. The boy begins to climb down the tree.

But he can't. He's stuck.

In his panic, there is nothing to do except call and hope he's heard.

'Yes, son?'

The answer comes back straight away. Of course they heard him.
Soon, his dad is beside him, showing him the way to get down. Putting the boy's feet on the correct branches. Step by step until, together, they reach the ground. Safely.

God's like that.
Step by step.
Together.
He comes to where we are,
wherever we are,
and shows us the way.
Leads the way.
Putting our feet where they should go.
Helping us out of whatever it is we can't escape.
Leading us to safety.
Of course he hears.

Father God
You hear when I call.
I know you do.
But sometimes I forget to call.
I get stuck.
And I forget to call.
I don't know the way.
And I forget to call.
Please help me not to forget.
Amen.

You have a Deliverer.
Me.
Do you know what that means?
It means you have a way out.
A way back.
You feel trapped:
Defined by your past.
Suffocated by your present.
Constricted by your circumstances.
It's scary, isn't it?
But I can bring you release.
I can bring you to safety.
Not necessarily by changing your circumstances
but by being with you in them.
Because I see you in them.
Even when you don't.
You are not your situation.
You're worth more than that.
Much more.
So let me keep you safe.
I'm right here with you.
You have a Deliverer.
Me.
My child; do you know what that means?
You have a Deliverer.

11

God *Is* My Refuge

He will cover you with his feathers, and under his wings you will find refuge...

Psalm 91:4

When my goddaughter, Charis, was about 5, a group of us went for a picnic. We went for a walk first and decided to climb to the top of a hill. It seemed like a good idea at the time. Reaching the top of the hill, we realized that previously we'd been sheltered. It was blowing a gale up there! We unpacked our sandwiches anyway and attempted to ignore the wind whipping our hair about and making us shiver. After not very long, I felt a wriggle beside me as Charis huddled into my side. I put my arm round her and tried to keep her warm as best I could. My best was not good enough, though. A few minutes later, she moved away from me. She didn't go far. Just far enough to bend her head to ground level.

Then, almost snake-like, and still clutching a half-eaten sandwich, she wriggled towards me.
She squirmed under my coat until she was, once again, sitting beside me.

But this time, she was even closer.
Hidden there, protected from the wind in every direction,
she snuggled in and carried on eating her sandwich.
Charis took the initiative where she could.
She really didn't like the wind.
She felt cold,
uncomfortable,
buffeted.
It was difficult.
So she did something about it.

Maybe there are things in your life that you really don't like.
You wish they weren't there.
But they are.
And they are difficult.
How about taking the initiative where you can?
By turning to God in it all.
So you're as close as can be.
Protected in every direction.
Safe in the storm.

'under his wings you will find refuge . . .'

Father God
The storms are raging.
I can feel them all around me, pressing in.
It's hard.
I need a place to go.
Somewhere safe.

Thank you that you are that place.
My shelter from the storm.
My hiding place.
Help me to stay close.
Amen.

You have a Refuge.
Me.
Do you know what that means?
It means you have a shelter.
And do you know what that means?
It means you're covered.
Everywhere you go,
everything you do,
every situation you face,
I'm covering you.
Protecting you.
Sheltering you.
So be sheltered.
Take refuge.
In me.
I'm here.
Run to me.
Hide yourself in me.
I'm right here.
Waiting for you.
Waiting to welcome you,
to protect you from life's batterings,
to keep you safe.

Waiting to catch you in my arms and whisper:
You have a Refuge.
Me.
My child; do you know what that means?
You have a Refuge.

12

God *Is* My Shield

How often I have wanted to gather your children together as a hen protects her chicks beneath her wings, but you wouldn't let me.

Luke 13:34 (NLT)

I needed to do a bit of shopping. As I was about to go out, my 5-year-old niece caught my attention: 'Can I come?' I explained to her that I was only going food shopping. She'd probably get fed up. And anyway, I wouldn't be long. She'd be better off not coming.

She thought about this. Then she said, 'Can I come?'

So she came. The shopping took longer than it would have done had I been alone. But it was more *fun* than had I been alone. Rather than grabbing what I needed, paying for it and leaving, as quickly as possible, I shopped at her pace.

Which meant stopping and giggling at a funny-shaped potato, noticed even though potatoes were not on my list. I'd have missed it if it hadn't been just at Abigail's eye level. 'Look!' as I went to walk on, 'That potato has a funny nose!'

Which meant, at the end, putting a small item in a separate bag because 'I can help carry our shopping'.

Which meant surprising her later with the little treat I knew she'd seen but hadn't noticed me sneak through at the checkout.

Abigail didn't mind where I was going.
She asked if she could come before she even knew where I was going.
She just wanted to be with me.
And she wanted to help.
Can I come?

Abbie is not the only one who says, 'Can I come?'
God says it too.

Can I come?
Will you take me with you?

Father God
You like my company?
You want to spend time with me?
You want to help me?
Thank you.
I know I turn you down sometimes.
Maybe I think you won't want to bother with me.
Not really.
Or that you won't be interested in my life.
Not really.

I forget that I'm wrong.
Wherever I go or am, you always say:
'Can I come?'
Help me to reply 'yes, please'.
Every time.
Amen.

You have a Shield.
Me.
Do you know what that means?
It means you can use me.
I can help.
All you have to do is take me with you.
Hold me out in front.
I'll lead you.
Will you choose to let me?
Will you choose to remember I'm there?
Choose to bring me into your life and days?
I'd like you to.
I'll never say no, but you need to say yes.
It's your choice.
Take me with you.
As you live your life,
protect yourself,
by letting me be there.
Be aware of me.
You can hold on to me anytime you like.
And hold me out in front.
I'll clear the way ahead.
But you need to trust me.

By intentionally taking me along.
You have a Shield.
Me.
My child; do you know what that means?
You have a Shield.

13

God *Is* My Salvation

> [Jesus said] *My prayer is not that you take them out of the world but that you protect them from the evil one.*
>
> John 17:15

'I'll try, but no guarantees.'

These words have been said to me many times.
Occasionally by a friend or someone I might have asked for a favour:
'I'll try, but no guarantees.'

Often – and more crucially – by a surgeon in a hospital.
Many times, faced with scan results which show one of my (non-malignant) tumours has grown and needs to be operated on, the news is accompanied by a surgeon uttering:

'I'll do my best to remove the tumour without causing other nerve damage; I'll try, but no guarantees.'

And they do try. Every time. Often, they succeed. But sometimes, due to position and location of the tumour, other nerve damage is caused. Not because the surgeon is

not being careful. But because the surgeon is working with
conditions beyond their control.

No guarantees.

God is different.
Nothing is beyond his control.
Nothing.
Even when it seems that way.
God is God.
You are not.
Which is a good thing.
And God, who is far beyond the constricts of time,
sees the end from the beginning.
He also sees the present.
Which is why he can say you're safe.
Guaranteed.

Father God
Thank you for keeping me safe.
Even when I don't feel safe,
I can know I am.
Because you guarantee it.
Always.
Amen.

You have Salvation.
Me.
Do you know what that means?
It means you're safe.

Safe now, because your future is secure
in me.
Victory is not far off.
Eternal victory, which starts now.
Every situation you face,
you can overcome.
You really can,
because you're safe.
In me.
Tough times will come.
There will be days when life is hard.
Dark days.
Difficult days.
But they are not impossible days.
Victory is at hand.
You're safe.
So turn to me through the
pain or fear or bewilderment.
Because I am your security,
your safety,
your victory.
You have Salvation.
Me.
My child; do you know what that means?
You have Salvation.

14

God *Is* My Stronghold

My grace is sufficient for you, for my power is made perfect in weakness.

2 Corinthians 12:9

'I can't do it.' I looked down the length of the parallel bars in front of me. They seemed to stretch for miles. At the end was a physiotherapist, encouraging me: 'I think you can.'

On the floor each side were protective mats, in case I fell. When I fell, more like. My legs were so weak. Even sitting, as I was, in a wheelchair at one end of the bars, I knew it. I knew by the way my feet, unbidden, slipped off the footrests and my legs were unable to lift them back again. I knew by the way my legs trembled from the exertion of sitting. I knew because my legs had become so thin after months in hospital that standing, let alone walking, would surely snap them in two.

And yet: 'I think you can.'

Did she really think I could? I raised my eyes to hers. She really thought I could. Gripping the bars tightly, I hauled myself shakily to my feet. My legs did not snap.

'I think you can.'
Maybe she was right. I moved my right foot forward. Then my left.
'I think you can.'
Right. Left. Right. Left. Slowly, yet undeniably, I made my way along the bars.
And I did not fall.

We have a God who believes in us.
With confidence.
Who is always right.

'I can't do it.'

I think you can.

'I'm too weak.'

No, you're not.

'I'll mess it up.'

No, you won't.

'I'll fall.'

Maybe.
Maybe not.
And, if you do, I'll catch you.

'I'm not worth it.'

No, you're not.
You are more than worth it.

Father God
When I am weak, you are strong.
Help me to trust your strength,
rather than my weakness.
I look to you
and dare to believe you believe in me.
I look away
and doubt.
Help me to keep my eyes on you.
You think I can . . .
Amen.

You have a Stronghold.
Me.
Do you know what that means?
It means you have a place where
you are believed in.
I don't doubt you.
I believe in you.
Even when you don't believe in yourself.

Especially when you don't believe in yourself.
And it means you have a place where
you are defended.
I defend you.
I protect you.
Even when you think you're not worth it.
Especially when you think you're not worth it.
Because you're worth it to me.
You're always worth it.
You have a Stronghold.
Me.
My child; do you know what that means?
You have a Stronghold.

Part 3

The Lord Is My Shepherd

Psalm 23:1: 'The Lord is my shepherd; I have all that I need' (NLT).

Please take all your belongings with you when you leave the train.

That's what the announcement often says as a train approaches a station, and people duly check they have everything with them before they disembark and hurry off into whatever the day holds.

Different destinations – places, reasons, lives – but all checking they have their belongings with them.
Ensuring they have all they need.

What about you?
As you step into your weeks, days, moments?
Do you check you have everything, as you hurry through life?
Because the Lord is your shepherd, you have all that you need.

It's yours to take.

Please take all you're equipped with as you go through life.

All God has given you.
All you need.

'The LORD is my shepherd . . .'

Isaiah 40:11: 'He tends his flock like a shepherd: he gathers the lambs in his arms and carries them close to his heart'.

'. . . I have all that I need.'

15

He Lets Me Rest in Green Meadows

As Jesus and his disciples were on their way, he came to a village where a woman named Martha opened her home to him. She had a sister called Mary, who sat at the Lord's feet listening to what he said. But Martha was distracted by all the preparations that had to be made. She came to him and asked, 'Lord, don't you care that my sister has left me to do the work by myself? Tell her to help me!' 'Martha, Martha,' the Lord answered, 'you are worried and upset about many things, but few things are needed – or indeed only one. Mary has chosen what is better, and it will not be taken away from her.'

Luke 10:38–42

My sister was 4 when she started school. At the end of the morning, walking home with our mum, she announced: 'I've done school now.' When she realized she needed to go back to school the next day, she was most affronted. 'But I've done school.' The next day, too: 'But I've done school.'

The youngest of four, she saw her older sisters go to school every day. She could have thought it was a natural thing to do. But she didn't. It was OK for them to go to school, but not her. She didn't need that.

She did keep going to school. She hardly missed a day, which probably contributed to the fact that she did very well.
School was not a one-off.
There is so much a 4-year-old must learn, to be as best prepared as possible for life ahead. Going to school once can't possibly achieve that.

Matthew 11:28: 'Come to me, all you who are weary and burdened, and I will give you rest.'

Rest is not a one-off.
But how often we think we don't need it.
Or we've done it.
Or it's for other people.
'But I've done rest.'
Well, do it again.
Life is so busy these days,
or stressful,
or hard.
There's so much to be done.
Or not done.
Getting through each day is an achievement.
And making rest a one-off rarity is not good preparation for the days and weeks ahead.
'But I've done rest.'
Well, do it again.

Father God
I have so much to do.

I'm so busy.
My diary is bulging.
Even when it's not,
I can't seem to stop finding
things to do.
Or not do.
Help me to factor in rest.
And to know it's OK.
Amen.

'The LORD is my shepherd; I have all that I need.
He lets me rest in green meadows . . .' (NLT).
He lets me rest?
That can't be right.
I have to keep going, be busy, do things for him.
He lets me rest?
No, it can't mean me.
This must be talking about other people – they can rest.
I have to keep going, be busy, do things for him.
He lets me rest?
Well, it does say 'me', but
surely it can't be right.
I have to keep going, be busy, do things for him.
How am I supposed to find the time to rest?
I'd feel so guilty.
There's so much to do.
I have to keep going, be busy, do things for him.
To be honest,
I could do with stopping sometimes.

But I remind myself:
'The LORD is my shepherd, I have all that I need.'

What about the next bit?
Why don't you remind yourself of that?

Because it's not for me.
I know that.
I've just said that.
I can't let myself rest.

I know you can't.
And I'm not asking you to.
Read it again.

'The LORD is my shepherd; I have all that I need.'

And the next bit.

'He lets me rest in green meadows . . .'

Now do you see?

I don't think I do.
'He lets me . . .'
Oh. It says 'he'.
Not me.
You let me rest?

I do. More than that, I want you to.

You need to.
Don't prohibit what I permit.
I let you rest.
You have all that you need.
I am your Shepherd.

16

He Leads Me beside Peaceful Streams

I am leaving you with a gift – peace of mind and heart. And the peace I give is a gift the world cannot give. So don't be troubled or afraid.

John 14:27 (NLT)

It was the day before Christmas. We'd managed to get all the family together under one roof, quite a feat for a large family which grows ever larger. The children were excited, dashing around, enjoying seeing their cousins. I was in the kitchen when my 5-year-old niece came up to me. She had a secret to tell.

'Aunty Memem; I went into your room, but I tiptoed in case there were any surprises you don't want me to see.'

I hadn't told her she had presents from me, but she went and had a little look anyway.

'I am leaving you with a gift – peace of mind and heart.'

There it is, loud and clear.

He gives us peace.
My niece didn't know she had a gift,
yet she looked anyway.
We know we have a peace present,
but how often we forget to look.
It's not hiding,
yet we miss it.
We miss peace.
We mourn its absence.
Yet it is not absent at all.

Father God
Peace is such a gift.
You give it to me.
Yet I forget the gift is for me.
I don't open it.
And I miss out.
In the turmoil of life
I miss the peace.
Help me not to miss it.
Please.
Amen.

'The LORD is my shepherd; I have all that I need.
. . . he leads me beside peaceful streams . . .' (NLT).
But the thing is, I'm not sure he does.
I know that sounds terrible.
But my life is anything but peaceful.
I dash from here to there,
one crisis to another,

busy, busy, busy.
He leads me beside peaceful streams?
I'll believe that when I see it.
I try to follow him, I really do.
So in that sense, he is leading me.
But peaceful streams?
They're nowhere to be seen.

Have you looked for them?

What?

Have you looked for peaceful streams?

Of course I have, Lord, but there aren't any.
I'm not complaining though.
I'm grateful for the life you've given me.
It's not peaceful, but that's OK.

No, it's not.

What?

It's not OK.
It's not OK that you miss the peace I give you.

It's not that I miss it. It's just not there.

It is there.

Is it?

Yes.
I always put peace on the path I lead you along.

Oh. So I do miss it. I walk right past peace. Every day.
But I don't see it.
And you're right.
It's not OK.
I miss peace.
I don't want to miss it.
Please help.

What did you do today?

Today was not great.
The train was late, and I stood waiting for it in the rain, thinking of what I was missing.

Oh. So you did think about peace!

Well, no. I meant the meeting I was missing, and the . . .

My child; as I led you through today,
I knew the train would be late.
Did you know that peaceful streams can look like late trains?
They can look like grabbing a cup of coffee.
They can look like . . .
I lead you beside peaceful streams.
You have all that you need.
I am your Shepherd.

17

He Renews My Strength

But those who hope in the LORD will renew their strength. They will soar on wings like eagles; they will run and not grow weary, they will walk and not be faint.

Isaiah 40:31

I stood in my cot. I was holding on to the bars, and I was crying. I was tired. I stood there, wailing, until someone came. Someone always came. They laid me down in the cot, tucked my blanket around me, and left me to sleep. Before long, I was standing in my cot. I was holding on to the bars, and I was crying. I was tired. Someone came. And they realized why this kept happening. I had learned how to stand up, but I didn't know how to lie back down again. Once standing, I was stuck. I couldn't stop standing. The next two or three times I was put to bed, I was gently restrained, my reins looped around my mattress.

I needed to learn the art of not standing up until I'd learned how to lie down.
It didn't take long.
Within a couple of days, the reins were redundant.
I'd learned how to lie down.

Like baby me, we need to learn to lie down.
To stop for a bit.
So that we can also stand.

Those who hope in the LORD will renew their strength.
You will lie down.
Those who hope in the LORD will soar on wings like eagles.
You will rest.
Those who hope in the LORD will run and not grow weary.
You will stand.
Those who hope in the LORD will walk and not be faint.
You will.

Father God
I'm tired.
But I don't know how to lie down.
I'm stuck.
I'm not sure I can go on.
I don't think I can face tomorrow.
Please help me lie down.
And be renewed.
Amen.

'The LORD is my shepherd; I have all that I need.
. . . He renews my strength' (NLT).
Every night, I fall asleep, exhausted.
When I eventually fall asleep.
Exhausted from the day,
exhausted from coping,

exhausted from smiling,
exhausted from pain –
and exhausted from hiding it –
exhausted from being exhausted.
My strength is gone.
And yet, when I wake in the morning, I
do it all again.
I worry that I won't be able to.
That one day, my strength will be gone.
Forever.
And I won't know how to get it back.

You don't need to do that.

What? Worry?

Well, yes; you don't need to worry.
Ever.
But I was thinking about knowing.
You don't need to know.
Because I know.
And that's all you need to know.
You can trust me.
All those days you've lived through?
I gave you the strength which carried you.
I gave you me.
I'm with you.
I was, I am and I will be.

You can go on.
We can.
Together.
I'll renew your strength.
You have everything you need.
I am your Shepherd.

18

He Guides Me along Right Paths

I will instruct you and teach you in the way you should go; I will counsel you with my loving eye on you.

Psalm 32:8

'Owen?!'

I cringed as my name rang out across the classroom. My maths teacher had just called out a sum and was expecting me to give the answer. I'm hopeless at maths. Before he'd even asked the question, my brain had frozen. And then he picked on me to answer. Why? Why not someone else, someone who did not get thrown into panic at the mere mention of maths? Why?

I knew why. It was because of my dad. My dad taught maths and was a colleague of my teacher. My teacher found it hard to believe that my dad and I could be so very different.

My sister, on the other hand, was good at maths. She'd inherited that from Dad. A real chip off the old block.

Dad was proud when she aced the exams I'd barely passed
and went on to study maths further.

Just as he was proud when I did well at English.
Just as he was proud when, following an operation which
left me unable to walk, I slowly learned to walk again.

My sister and I are different.
Dad knew that.
And it's OK.
People are different.
I'm not you.
You're not me.
God knows that.
And it's OK.

1 Corinthians 12:18: 'God has placed the parts in the body
[of Christ], every one of them, just as he wanted them to be.'

When we long to be someone else,
we reject who God made us to be.

Father God
I compare myself with others.
I do.
And I never come out favourably.
You don't compare me with others.
And I always come out favourably.
Help me to be more like you.
Please.
Amen.

'The LORD is my shepherd; I have all that I need.
. . . He guides me along right paths' (NLT).
I know I need a guide.
So often I stand at crossroads in my life.
I could go forwards, backwards, right, left.
But which is the right path?
I know I need a guide.
I believe I have a guide.
I do.
I know I'm not alone,
wandering into my tomorrows.
I have a guide.
Who knows my way.
But why would he bother with my way?
I don't understand.
And yet, I know.
I have a guide.

You do.
Always.
But you want to know why?
I'll tell you.
When you choose to
follow the right way,
walk in step with me,
live the life you have,
you bring honour to my name.
You do.
Following the right way,
even when it's hard,
honours me.

And yet, I see you worrying.
I see you looking around.
I see you thinking other people honour me more.
You're wrong.
You honour me.
When you let me show you the way,
and then walk with me in it,
you bring honour to my name.
You do.
I guide you along right paths.
You have everything you need.
I am your Shepherd.

19

Your Rod and Your Staff Protect and Comfort Me

For I hold you by your right hand – I, the LORD your God. And I say to you, 'Don't be afraid. I am here to help you.'

Isaiah 41:13 (NLT)

It wasn't yesterday, though it could have been. My first-ever brain scan. I remember the white gown I had to wear, the one with 'hospital' printed all over it. Not that there was any chance of me forgetting where I was. I'd been moved from clinic waiting room, to consulting room, to one ward, to another ward, and finally into the scanning department. I'd fumbled with the gown, trying to tie the enormous piece of material around me.

I shivered. It was so cold. My bare feet felt like blocks of ice. The radiographer opened a large brown door and beckoned me in. I just stood in the doorway. They expected me to lie down and go in that tunnel-shaped thing I could see? It dominated the room and yet at the same time seemed small. I wasn't even sure I'd fit in the tunnel.

I did fit in. I am tall, but the tunnel was longer. Every bit of me was hidden inside the scan machine. Except my feet. Those ice-cold feet.

Feet which felt a warm hand on them.

I couldn't see it as I lay there, head held immobile by a brace, encased in a tunnel so narrow my shoulders touched the sides. I could only feel the hand, but I knew who it was. My mum.

She'd promised to be there throughout the whole lengthy scan.

And she was.

Part of my foot wasn't icy cold.

However closed-off we feel, God is there.
And he's not going anywhere.
However cold we feel, God is there.
And he's not going anywhere.
In dark times, God is there.
And he's not going anywhere.

Psalm 139:12: 'Even the darkness will not be dark to you; the night will shine like the day, for darkness is as light to you.'

Father God
Darkness dominates,
presses in,
surrounds.
But it's not as bad as it could be,

because you are here.
And darkness is as light to you.
You see the way I can't.
Stay close.
Please.
I need you.
Amen.

'The LORD is my shepherd; I have all that I need.
. . . Your rod and your staff protect and comfort me' (NLT).
I wish the light wouldn't disappear sometimes.
But it does.
All is dark.
And I live in the shadows.
Shadows of things I cannot see.
Shadows of light extinguished.
Shadows of the unknown.
I live in the shadows.
And yet, as I gaze blindly into nothing,
reaching for something,
I am scared but unafraid.
I am nervous but
my reaching hands meet courage.
I realize,
and am comforted.
I hold on.
You are here.

I am.
Because you are.

I am the Light in your shadows.
The Light which never disappears.
Darkness all around but not within.
Light of presence.
Light of courage.
Light of assurance.
Light of comfort.
Light of hope.
Light of love.
Your reaching hands meet mine.
They meet me.
I reach for you, my child.
I find you.
And I hold on.
Always.
I protect and comfort you.
You have all that you need.
I am your Shepherd.

20

You Prepare a Feast for Me in the Presence of My Enemies

'Because he loves me,' says the LORD, 'I will rescue him; I will protect him, for he acknowledges my name. He will call on me, and I will answer him; I will be with him in trouble, I will deliver him and honour him.'

Psalm 91:14,15

'You'll get your head flushed down the toilet.'

That's what I remember being told about my new school. It's not what made me nervous – I was a nervous child anyway – but it certainly contributed to my general sense of terror at starting secondary school. I'd tried everything, even asking my aunty if I could run away and live with her. I promised I'd be helpful and look after my little cousins.

But the day came.
And I started secondary school.
I did not get my head flushed down the toilet.
I did get tripped over as I walked down the corridor.
I did get taunted.

I did get my chair pulled from underneath me just as I sat down.

I did get doors deliberately slammed in my face.

I did get mocked for wearing school uniform, for doing my homework, for speaking properly, for where I lived.

For anything, really.

When I was tripped over, I picked myself up and carried on walking.

When I was taunted and mocked, I didn't answer.

When the chair was pulled from under me, I got up from the floor.

Inside me, I cried, but I refused to let my tears show.

And, gradually, doors weren't slammed in my face.

People didn't bother mocking me.

Or at least not as frequently.

I don't kid myself they stopped because they decided I was all right after all.

They stopped because they did not get a reaction from me.

They gave up because I ignored them.

And the more I ignored them,

the less they bothered me.

2 Corinthians 4:17,18: 'For our present troubles are small and won't last very long. Yet they produce for us a glory that vastly outweighs them and will last forever! So we don't look at the troubles we can see now; rather, we fix our gaze on things that cannot be seen. For the things we see now will soon be gone, but the things we cannot see will last forever' (NLT).

Father God
With you on my side, I can face everything.
I can overcome anything.
I know I can,
but sometimes I look the wrong way.
Help me to focus on you and
all you offer.
Victory is mine
because of you.
Amen.

'The LORD is my shepherd; I have all that I need.
. . . You prepare a feast for me in the presence of my ene-
mies' (NLT).
I do have enemies.
And so many of them come from within.
Doubts, weaknesses, fears.
'I'm not good enough.'
'I'm pathetic.'
'I can't do this.'
'I must be a bad person.'
'I'm not worth believing in.'
What if these voices are true?
Maybe they are.
I need to run from them,
before they become my voice.
But they just won't go.
I can't make them leave.

Yes, you can.

Can I? How?

By making them leave by themselves.
I prepare a feast for you in the presence of your enemies.
Will you enjoy what I have prepared for you?
Come on.
Look, I'm pulling out a chair for you.
Sit down. Feast on the delights I've prepared.
Security, protection, comfort, light.
Come on, what are you waiting for?!

It's just that, well, THEY are still here.

Oh, don't let them stop you.
Ignore them.
You just focus on feasting on my delights.

OK, Lord, I'll try . . .
They've gone!

Of course they have.
I prepared your feast in their presence but, once they saw you enjoying it,
they knew they didn't stand a chance.
They might try to sneak back,
so don't stop feasting.
I prepare a feast for you in the presence of your enemies.
You have everything you need.
I am your Shepherd.

21

You Honour Me by Anointing My Head with Oil

. . . you are precious to me. You are honored, and I love you.

Isaiah 43:4b (NLT)

It was 4.30 a.m. on a Sunday morning. I was lying in my hospital bed, woken by the sunlight in my eyes. It was streaming through the window where the curtain didn't close. I'd been in hospital for six weeks now. Six weeks of a strange existence which was becoming alarmingly normal. I didn't want it to be normal. Especially not today. Normal on a Sunday, for me, meant going to church. And suddenly, I wanted my normal, more than anything. I wanted to go to church, and I lay there desperately wishing it were possible. Convincing myself I'd be able to walk as far as the car park. I, who at this stage struggled to even walk around my bed.

The sun moved round a bit. Now it was not fully in my eyes, but falling on my bed, too. Highlighting all the reasons I would not be going to church that day. Legs that didn't work, tubes attached to various machines and contraptions. No, I was stuck. As I looked at myself, a question

I've never asked before popped, unbidden, into my mind. *Why would God want your worship? Look at you. You're pathetic. Useless. You can hardly even move.*

A few months ago, I'd been teaching children at church about worship. Very simply, we'd learned that 'worship is doing what makes God happy'.

Now I couldn't do anything.
'Why would God want your worship?'
Then God stepped in with a question of his own.

Emily, what do you think was the biggest act of worship in the Bible?

I ran through some possibilities. Abraham being willing to offer his son? Daniel refusing to bow down to other gods? Mary being willing to accept the responsibility of being Jesus' mother?
All incredible.
Then I came to the cross.
And God said:

That's it.

Jesus.
Nailed to the cross.
Paralysed.
Unmoving
yet unwavering.

Steadfast in obedience to his Father.

Worship.

Hebrews 12:2: 'Because of the joy awaiting him, he endured the cross, disregarding its shame. Now he is seated in the place of honor beside God's throne' (NLT).

Father God
I am precious.
To you.
I am honoured.
Before you.
I am loved.
By you.
Thank you.
So much.
Amen.

'The LORD is my shepherd; I have all that I need.
. . . You honor me by anointing my head with oil' (NLT).
But that can't be right.
Only the most distinguished guests are anointed with oil.
It's wrong to anoint me.
I'm not a distinguished guest.
There's nothing special about me.

I'm glad you said that.
I do honour you.
I esteem you.

You are distinguished.
You are precious in my sight.
But sometimes I don't think you grasp quite how precious.
So let me tell you again . . .
Before I made anything,
I looked through time and space,
and I saw you.
Before I made anything,
I looked through time and space,
and I loved what I saw.
I loved you.
Before you'd done a single thing.
I loved you.
I still love you.
You're my distinguished guest.
Always.
Never believe you're not wanted.
Never believe you're not lovable.
Never believe you're not precious.
I honour you by anointing your head with oil.
You have all that you need.
I am your Shepherd.

Part 4

I AM

When one of my nieces learned to say her name, it was, at times, confusing for her. She didn't understand the difference between *who* she was and *what* she was. If asked her name, she would reply, 'Elianne.' All well and good but, if called a 'giggle-pot' when tickled, a 'funny-bunny' when she said something amusing or even a 'beautiful princess' when she wore a particularly nice dress, she would become quite indignant. 'I'm NOT a giggle-pot/funny-bunny/princess.'

When asked, in that case, what was she?
'I'm a Elianne.'
Full stop.
End of discussion.
As if that one word explained what she was.

In Exodus, chapter 3, we see Moses asking God for his name.
The answer?
'I AM WHO I AM.'

I imagine that was as confusing for Moses as for people to whom Elianne declared, 'I'm a Elianne.'

It is as I get to know Elianne more, to watch her grow, to learn what interests her, to spend time with her that I come to understand what makes Elianne, Elianne.
In the same way, it is as we get to know God more that we can begin to understand what makes God – the 'I AM' – God.

Throughout the Old Testament, we see God trying to reveal what he is and people just not getting it. But God (being God) doesn't give up. He comes to earth as a person. As Jesus.
The human face of 'I AM'.
And Jesus, the God-Man, expands on the I AM of the Old Testament.

The New Testament records seven 'I AMs' Jesus spoke.
As we consider each, may we come into a deeper relationship with our God, the great 'I AM'.

John 10:30: '[Jesus said] I and the Father are one.'
John 14:11: '[Jesus said] I am in the Father and the Father is in me'.

22

I AM the Light of the World

The light shines in the darkness, and the darkness has not overcome it.

John 1:5

I wonder if you've ever tried to hide light? I have.

When I was growing up, I loved to read. Every night at bed-time, I was allowed half an hour or so to read before I had to turn my light out. After half an hour, I would invariably find myself halfway through a grippingly exciting chapter. What to do? Get a torch, of course! So, I would dutifully switch my light off at the allotted time and, not so dutifully, switch my torch on. I would hide under the covers with book and torch until I'd finished the chapter . . . or the next . . . or the next.

I thought I was very clever, and it wasn't until years later, when I happened to mention this to my mum, that I realized I'd fooled no one. 'I know,' she said. 'I could see the light shining under your door.'

Darkness cannot overcome light. Sometimes we need to remind ourselves of that.

When dark times come, Jesus is the light of the world.
When we have problems within our families, Jesus is the light of the world.
When we are afraid of tomorrow, Jesus is the light of the world.
When we feel that there's no point in going on, Jesus is the light of the world.
When we wonder if God really cares, Jesus is the light of the world.

It's just before midnight on Christmas Eve. When people arrive and walk into church, there are no lights on. It is pitch-black.
Then someone lights a candle.
Just one candle.
Suddenly, it's not pitch-black any more. All eyes turn towards that candle and focus on it.
Beforehand, everyone was looking at their own patch of darkness, but now we're all looking in the same direction.
No one ignores the candle and sits staring into a dark corner instead.
Yes, the dark corners are there.
But all focus is on the light.

There will be difficult times in life.
There will be trials, worries, doubts . . .
but we can choose to focus, not on the dark corners, but on the light.
On Jesus, the light of the world.

Lord God
When life is dark, help me turn to you.
When I'm lonely, sad, frustrated, doubting,
help me turn to you.
I'm sorry for the times I focus on the dark things in life
instead of you.
Thank you that you never turn your light off,
and that nothing and no one can hide your light.
Thank you that Jesus said, 'I AM the Light of the World.'
Amen.

John 8:12: '[Jesus said] I am the light of the world.'
I am the one who overcame all the powers of darkness,
and I did it for you.
I did it because
I want you to know the light of belonging
instead of the darkness of loneliness.
I want you to know the light of identity
instead of the darkness of insecurity.
I want you to know the light of experiencing God's love,
instead of the darkness of not really believing that
God loves you.
I am the Light of your World.

23

I AM the Way, the Truth and the Life

Search me, God, and know my heart; test me and know my anxious thoughts. See if there is any offensive way in me, and lead me in the way everlasting.

Psalm 139:23,24

'I know where I'm going.'

Perhaps we all recognize these words. How many times have we been on a car journey, discovered we're hopelessly lost and, after pleading with the driver to stop and ask for directions, been told: 'I know where we are. I'm sure I'll recognize somewhere in a minute.'

Why do we have such a dislike of asking for directions? Of admitting we're lost? Of asking for help?

Driving along, my sister noticed we were low on petrol. 'Don't worry,' said her husband. 'There's a petrol station a few miles down the road, we'll stop there.'

As it happened, we stopped, due to an empty tank, sooner than anticipated – on a very busy road. Cars were whizzing past, narrowly avoiding us, and all we could do was sit there and try not to panic. Eventually, when panic abated, we realized we'd come to a stop near a car park. It looked deserted but, in the end, for want of any other options, my sister leaned out of the window and called, 'Help!'

Straight away came an answering shout. We explained our dilemma and the man went to get some petrol, put it in our car for us, directed us to the nearest petrol station so we could fill our tank, met us at the station and then drove, so we could follow, back to the busy road.

Stuck on the road.
Life seems to stop.
Everyone else looks busy, content, managing fine.
And you're just stuck.
In a rut.
Not moving.
Stuck on the road.

Well, God sees.
God listens.
He hears you calling 'help'.
And, like the man in the car park, he answers straight back:

Let me get you what you need, give you what you need, show you what you need, lead you where you need to go.

Lord God
I'm sorry for the times when I try to go it alone.
I always get stuck.

Thank you that I can depend on you in everything.

Thank you that you know where I'm going.

Please help me remember to call out to you before I get stuck next time.

Thank you that Jesus said, 'I AM the Way, the Truth and the Life.'

Amen.

John 14:6: '[Jesus said] I am the way and the truth and the life.'

I am the one who overcame all the powers of falsehood and lack of direction,

and I did it for you.

I did it because

I want you to know the reality of knowing God

instead of the pretence that you can manage perfectly well on your own.

I want you to know the satisfaction of having a purpose for existing

instead of the unhappiness of not really knowing why you are here.

I want you to know the comfort of being dependent on God instead of the pressure of trying to go it alone.

I am your Way, your Truth and your Life.

24

I AM the Door

Here I am! I stand at the door and knock. If anyone hears my voice and opens the door, I will come in ...

Revelation 3:20

When I was about 12, I longed to go horse-riding. I'd only ever ridden ponies on the beach or at the fair, but my grandfather had passed on a love of horses to my mum who, in turn, passed on a similar enthusiasm to me.

One summer, Mum told me she'd booked me in for a five-day horse-riding course. What a lovely surprise. I was ecstatic and very excited. The course was to take place at a riding school in the country and a minibus would transport participants. We were to catch the minibus at a local school and would be taken back there at the end of the morning.

That first morning, about ten of us piled into the bus after our parents had dropped us off, looking forward to the day ahead and chattering non-stop. I had a lovely time and couldn't wait to go back the next day.

The next day, however, something had changed. No longer were we a happy group who were all getting along fine. Somewhere along the line, a couple of boys decided they wanted to be 'top dog'. They also decided I was to be the runt of the litter.

For the rest of the week, my happiness at going horse-riding was tarnished by the taunts and sly comments from these boys.

One day, we were taking our ponies back to the stable before getting on the bus to come home. For some reason, I took longer than the others and was last to reach the bus. The door was open and, as I was about to climb in, one of the boys called out, 'Shut the door in front of you.'

Shut the door in front of you. It seems ludicrous, doesn't it? Why would anyone shut the door in front of themselves? But sometimes we do.

We shut the door between us and God – slam!
And why?

Maybe we're scared. Slam.
Maybe we're ashamed. Slam.
Maybe we're too self-reliant. Slam.
Maybe we're tired. Slam.
Maybe we're busy. Slam.
Maybe we don't think we're worth God's attention. Slam.

Maybe . . . Slam!
Maybe . . . Slam!
Maybe . . . Slam!

Maybe we will keep on shutting the doors.
Keep on blocking God out.
Or maybe,
just maybe,
we could open the door and throw away the key.

Lord God
I'm sorry for the times when I shut you out.
I don't know why I do it, but I do it.
I slam the door in your face.
It hurts but I do it anyway.
You know how many doors there are in my life,
but I want you to share everything about me.
Please help me have the courage to open my doors to you.
Thank you that you're waiting on the other side.
Thank you that Jesus said, 'I AM the Door.'
Amen.

John 10:9: '[Jesus said] I am the door' (NKJV).
I am the one who overcame all the powers of doubt,
and I did it for you.
I did it because
I want you to know the adventure of a future with me
instead of the confusion of a life that has no real meaning.
I want you to know the relief of opening all the doors in
your life to me

instead of the anxiety of secretly slamming some of them shut in my face.

I want you to know the joy that can be yours when you open those doors and find me waiting for you on the other side, instead of never knowing what would have happened if you'd only trusted me enough to open them.

I am your Door.

25

I AM the Good Shepherd

See, I have engraved you on the palms of my hands . . .

Isaiah 49:16

In the film *Home Alone*, 8-year-old Kevin accidently gets left at home when his family forget to take him on holiday. At first, Kevin quite enjoys being 'home alone' but he soon realizes that being on his own is not as much fun as he'd thought.

Sometimes, being on your own is not fun.

Do you sometimes feel like that?
Do you feel, like Kevin, that you've been forgotten?
Jesus told a story for you (see Matthew 18; Luke 15).

A shepherd had 100 sheep, then one went missing. The shepherd is faced with a choice. Concentrate on the ninety-nine, or the one? Except it's not really a choice. The man's flock will not be complete if one is missing. So he goes looking for it.

He searches everywhere for that sheep.
He finds that sheep.
And he brings that sheep home.

Jesus is that shepherd.
And you are that sheep.
Jesus searches for you.
Searches for you until he finds you.

Now, let's look at this from the sheep's point of view.

One day, she decides to go exploring. She never intends to go out of sight of her shepherd, it just kind of happens. And then it just seems easier to continue rather than go back. So she does. Then, gradually, she realizes she is utterly lost. She has no idea how to get back to her shepherd. For a while, she dashes around in every direction, trying desperately to get back on track, hoping she'll find her way back to her shepherd. But, finally, she is forced to give up. She hopes someone will notice she's missing but she's out of options. She's been 'running on empty' for a while, and she just can't do it any more.

So, she crawls into a hollow,
and hides.
She just can't find her way back to her shepherd,
so she hides.
She's lost.
She's hungry.

She's cold.
So she hides.
People pass by, but no one notices her.
Then it's night-time, and no one passes by.
It's dark.
She's scared.
She's alone.
So she hides.
And then,
in the midst of her fear and loneliness,
her shepherd comes.

Lord God
I don't like it when I'm missing.
You don't like it when I'm missing.
It amazes me that you think I'm worth searching for.
But you do.
Thank you that you search for me,
again and again,
every time I lose my way.
Thank you that you persevere.
Thank you that you come.
Thank you that you always find me.
Thank you that Jesus said, 'I AM the Good Shepherd.'
Amen.

John 10:11: '[Jesus said] I am the good shepherd.'
I am the one who overcame all the powers of despair,
and I did it for you.

I did it because

I want you to know the security of sharing your life with me, instead of the deep-down fear and uncertainty of excluding me from it.

I want you to know the protection and care I long to give you,

instead of refusing to come to me and let me help.

I want you to know that I value you so much,

instead of you sometimes feeling no one would notice if you weren't here.

I am your Good Shepherd.

26

I AM the Vine

How good and pleasant it is when God's people live together in unity!

Psalm 133:1

Some years ago, the amount of rainfall in the north of England was the leading news story in the UK. There had been unprecedented flooding in Cumbria, resulting in bridges collapsing. People had to move out of their homes as the flood waters rose and, when they were able to move back, found damp, damaged rooms. The number of insurance claims predicted was phenomenal.

One local man interviewed said that they lived on a network of rivers. They relied on bridges to get around. Without bridges, life would be very difficult.

I think that man summed up the Christian life.

They lived on a network of rivers.

In other words, the area contains lots of rivers doing their own thing. Sometimes meeting, sometimes not.

The church contains lots of Christians doing their own thing. Sometimes meeting, sometimes not.

They relied on bridges to get around.

In other words, the area cannot function as it should without bridges. One shopkeeper interviewed said that business was down 30 per cent, as many of his customers could only reach his shop via bridges. The shopkeeper lost out, and the customers lost out. Everyone lost out.

The church cannot function as it should without bridges. Bridges between people, between groups, between communities. Without bridges, everyone loses out.

Without bridges, life would be very difficult.

Without the bridges, life in that region still goes on. People manage, find other ways of doing things, work round the lack of bridges – but it's not easy.

Without bridges in the church, life still goes on. People manage, find other ways of doing things, go the long way round rather than building bridges between people, groups, communities – but it's not easy. More importantly, it's not living as God intended his church to live. He wants a united, vibrant, 'together' church. And he wants to help us build those bridges.

Remember the scene from *A Christmas Carol*, where Scrooge is outside in the cold, looking through a window at the Christmas celebrations and laughter going on inside?

Do you sometimes feel like that?

You look at other people, other Christians, and think you can never be a part of what they're enjoying?

Build bridges. Start today. He'll help you.

That's why Jesus said, 'I am the Vine.'

Lord God
Thank you that, when I turned to you, I became part of your family.
I love being part of your family.
But I have to confess; sometimes
the other people in your family
drive me crazy!
Help me to build bridges with them, instead of always going the long way round.
Help me to accept and be accepted.
Thank you that you are a master bridge-builder.
Thank you that Jesus said, 'I AM the Vine.'
Amen.

John 15:1: '[Jesus said] I am the true vine'.
I am the one who overcame all the powers of disunity,
and I did it for you.

I did it because

I want you to know the pleasure of being included instead of the misery of not belonging.

I want you to know the joy of being accepted instead of the pain of rejection.

I want you to know the happiness of living within the circle of my love instead of the loneliness of staying outside and looking in.

I am your Vine.

27

I AM the Bread of Life

I am the living bread that came down from heaven. Whoever eats this bread will live for ever. This bread is my flesh, which I will give for the life of the world.

John 6:51

One bitterly cold day, I was walking as fast as I could. I had a train to catch and wanted to shelter in the station while I waited. As I neared the station, I saw a man sitting against a wall, huddled under thin blankets. I smiled at him as I hurried by. He smiled back. Then I was in the relative warmth of the station, queuing, buying my ticket, checking which platform my train came into.

I looked at the clock. There was still time. I retraced my steps to the man I'd been thinking about ever since I'd hurried past him. It was such a cold day. Perhaps he'd like a hot drink.

'Would you like a drink?'
His response surprised me.
'Coffee; milk and two sugars.'

Afterwards, I asked myself why his response had struck me.

It was because of what it lacked.
It lacked suspicion.
It lacked *why would you offer me that?*
It lacked *are you sure you have time to bother?*
What it didn't lack was denial.
'Coffee; milk and two sugars.'
Acceptance of his own situation.
And acceptance of mine.
He couldn't get himself a drink.
I could get him a drink.
'Coffee; milk and two sugars.'

A genie offers a man three wishes.
'Well,' says the man, 'for my first wish I'd like a box of chocolates that never gets empty, however many chocolates I eat.'
'Done!' Says the genie. 'What about your other wishes?'
'I'll have two more never-ending boxes of chocolates, please.'

Are we really so different from the man in the joke?

Jesus tells us in John 6:35: 'I am the bread of life. Whoever comes to me will never go hungry'. But then, like the man in the joke, we begin to doubt.
We think we need a back-up plan.
Just in case.

So we take our eyes off the one who is giving us all we need, in order to search for other ways of getting what we need.

Just in case.

And then we're caught between a rock and a hard place.
We know Jesus is offering all we need, but something prevents us from accepting it,
prevents us from not trying to do it ourselves,
prevents us from just saying,
'Thanks.'

'I am the bread of life. Whoever comes to me will never go hungry'.

It's not complicated.
It's not rocket science.
'Coffee; milk and two sugars.'
Just take it.

Matthew 10:8: '[Jesus said] Freely you have received'.

When Jesus gave himself,
bruised,
broken,
dying on the cross . . .
He was thinking of you.
He was thinking of me.
He was thinking of all the people who would ever need sustaining in a way that they couldn't manage by themselves.
The people who are marginalized.
The people who are depressed.
The people who are ill.

The people who are struggling.
The people like you.
The people like me.

'Coffee; milk and two sugars.'

'I am the bread of life. Whoever comes to me will never go hungry'.

Lord God
Sometimes I'm not very good at taking from you.
You always offer me the best.
Always.
But I still think my way is better.
I do my own thing, just in case.
I'm sorry.
I do know that your way is by far the best.
Help me to remember I don't have to manage by myself.
Ever.
Thank you that you're always here, offering me your best.
Help me to take it.
Thank you that Jesus said, 'I AM the Bread of Life.'
Amen.

John 6:35: '[Jesus said] I am the bread of life.'
I am the one who overcame all the powers of hopelessness, and I did it for you.
I did it because
I want you to know the contentment of relying on me in everything

instead of the distress of trying to work it all out for yourself.
I want you to know how exciting your life will be if you share it with me;
all you have to do is give me the chance to show you.
I want you to know that I will provide everything you need;
all you have to do is allow me to do it.
I am your Bread of Life.

28

I AM the Resurrection and the Life

If anyone is in Christ, the new creation has come: the old has gone, the new is here!

2 Corinthians 5:17

I was walking my dog in the park when I noticed a large rock. There was a plaque on the rock, stating it had been placed to mark the year 2000. The rock looked fine, not out of place in its surroundings, quite a good way for the park to mark this special occasion.

A few weeks later, I saw that a low, wooden railing had been placed around the rock, and the grass within the railing had been covered with wood chippings. This added to the effect, making the rock more of a feature.

Not long afterwards, I saw the area had been vandalized. The railing had been broken and the ground around the rock trampled on. Soon, the railing and wood chips were removed.

So now the rock was back to square one. Actually, back to before square one. Now it was surrounded by mud, not grass. It looked quite bleak and forlorn until I noticed a little green shoot. Then another. Then another. Someone had planted seeds around that rock. They'd taken a while to come, but the wait was worth it.

Over the next few days, all around the rock, flowers were bursting into glorious colours.
Bursting into life.
And the rock looked more beautiful than ever before.

Life can be a bit like that rock.

For a while, you are going along just fine. Then something, maybe a promotion at work, a new house, something else, makes life even better. Like the wooden railing. And then, maybe things aren't so good, after all. The promotion at work means more pressure and stress. The new house means a bigger mortgage. Whatever you're focusing on loses some of its appeal. It's not so good any more. It has been spoiled, vandalized.

And then life is bleak.
You can't make it better.
You can't do it on your own.
You need someone else to plant the seeds.
That's when Jesus comes.
And Jesus cares.
He doesn't want your life to be bleak.
So he plants the seeds.
His seeds.

And makes them grow.
Until your life is better and more beautiful than before.

'If anyone is in Christ, the new creation has come . . .'

Lord God
I am like that rock.
I'm fine.
Improving, even.
And then I realize I'm not.
I'm not fine.
I'm not improving.
I'm just bleak.
Empty.
You know what that's like – you were empty on the cross.
You actually chose to be empty, so I could be made beautiful.
Thank you.
I want you to make me beautiful for you.
Please come and plant your seeds in my life.
Thank you that you love me enough to want the best for me.
Thank you that Jesus said, 'I AM the Resurrection and the Life.'
Amen.

John 11:25: '[Jesus said] I am the resurrection and the life.'
I am the one who overcame all the powers of death,
and I did it for you.
I did it so you can have eternal life.

I did it because you are precious to me.
I did it because I want you to know
how much I love you.
With me, each day is beautiful.
I am your Resurrection and your Life.

Part 5

Echoes from the Cross

I don't remember everything my granny ever said to me, but I do remember the last.

As she lay, dying, in hospital, she spoke. At this stage, speaking was not easy for her, but she had something important she wanted to say:

'The next one should be Esther.'

She meant I should write a book about the biblical Queen Esther.
Her final words.
I took them to heart, and my next book was indeed about Esther.

A person's final words can be significant.

What about Jesus?

The words he said as he hung, dying, on the cross.

Are they significant?
Does the echo of them still speak to us today?

Isaiah 53:3a: 'He was despised and rejected by mankind, a man of suffering, and familiar with pain.'

And yet, in that suffering and pain and rejection, he spoke.
He spoke to you.
He spoke to me.

A person's final words can be significant.

29

Father, Forgive

Bear with each other and forgive one another if any of you has a grievance against someone. Forgive as the Lord forgave you.

Colossians 3:13

I speak sign language. Not fluently, but I can get by. A wonderful thing about sign language is that children can learn it even before they can talk. So, long before they were able to utter 'thank you', my nieces and nephews were able to say it in sign language. That was the first sign they learned. Closely followed by 'sorry'! To sign 'sorry' in sign language, make a clenched fist and rub it in a small circle on your chest. The children soon learned to say this in response to 'What do you say . . .?'!

Josiah, however, put his own slant on it. At nearly 2 years old, rather than put his hand to his own chest, he would toddle over to the person he was apologizing to and rub a circle on their chest instead.

In other words, he was rubbing away the hurt or anger or unfairness they were feeling.

In a very child-like way, he was showing that it is not always easy to forgive.

It hurts.

Hurt that can need another's hand to soothe.

2 Kings 20:5: 'I have heard your prayer and seen your tears; I will heal you.'

God reaches down to us in our hurt,
stays with us in our hurt,
and gently wipes it away.

Lord Jesus
Sometimes the hurt I feel seems unbearable.
As though my chest will explode.
No one understands.
No one, except you.
Thank you that you come to me.
Stay with me in my hurting.
And wipe away my tears.
Amen.

The cry echoes from the cross down through the ages,
'Father, forgive them'.[1]
It is a triumphant cry, for
it is a genuine cry.

Forgiveness is possible.
More than that, it is attainable.
'Father, forgive them'.

Oh, Father of all forgiveness,
help me catch hold of that echo.
Its love,
its genuineness.
And, in doing so, realize that
I don't have to do it alone.
The strength of every echo is
its source.
The ability to truly forgive comes from
you.
Help me to listen to your echo.
All it means,
all it stands for.
Enable me to let it resound into my life and days.
May I never let your echo fade.

'Father, forgive them'.

30

Today You Will Be with Me in Paradise

The LORD himself goes before you and will be with you; he will never leave you nor forsake you. Do not be afraid; do not be discouraged.

Deuteronomy 31:8

Today was not going well. All alone, I sat down and opened my lunch box. I wished I didn't have to be at school. And now it was lunchtime. Lunch break always lasted forever when I spent it on my own, surrounded by groups of people. I picked at my sandwich, then reached for another. It was as I did so that I saw a piece of card nestled amongst my lunch. I pulled out a small, light green rectangle. In the bottom right-hand corner was a picture of a little mouse. Above it, in my mum's handwriting, were the words; 'Dear Em, I love you, Mum xxx'. A lump came to my throat, and my eyes filled with tears. I didn't feel so alone any more.

Matthew 28:20: 'I am with you always, to the very end of the age.'

Jesus promises that we never need to feel alone.

He's here. Wherever we are.

I am with you
always;
you're not alone.

Even when things go wrong?

I am with you
always;
you're not alone.

When even I don't like me?

I am with you
always;
you're not alone.

When I'm where I don't want to be?

I am with you
always;
you're not alone.

When I don't think I can take any more?

I am with you
always;
you're not alone.

When I . . .

Yes.
I am with you.
Always.

Lord Jesus
Even when I feel alone,
I'm not.
Even when I'm by myself,
or lonely in a crowd,
I'm not alone.
You are with me.
Right here.
Wherever I am.
Thank you.
Amen.

The cry echoes from the cross down through the ages,
'today you will be with me'.[1]
It is a reassuring cry for
it is a genuine cry.
I am not alone.
His presence is promised.
Every second.
'Today you will be with me'.
Today.
Now.
Always.
Promised presence.
Present presence.
'Today you will be with me'.

Oh, Father of ever-presence,
help me catch hold of that echo.
Its love,
its genuineness,
and, in doing so, realize again that
I am not alone.
The strength of every echo is
its source.
I am not alone because
you are here.
Right here.
Right now.
Help me to listen to your echo.
All it means,
all it stands for.
Enable me to let it resound into my life and days.
May I never let your echo fade.

'Today you will be with me'.

31

Woman, Here Is Your Son

What can I offer the L<small>ORD</small> for all he has done for me?
Psalm 116:12 (<small>NLT</small>)

I was with my sister and her family. It was a Saturday and,
pocket money clutched in their hands, the children went
off to the shop with their dad. When they came back, they
showed me what they'd bought; some sweets. I realized they
had not quite spent all their money and assumed they'd
put the rest in their money-saving jar. Then, out of the
bag came something else. A little packet of sweets. 'Aunty
Memem, we bought these sweets for you.' They had spent
all their money after all.

Having money to buy sweets is an exciting treat for the
children. It supersedes everything else in their thinking.
Or so I thought.

'Aunty Memem, we bought these sweets for you.'

They'd thought of others. They'd thought of me.

Thanking them, I put the sweets on the table. I'd open
them later.

Eyes looked at the sweets.

After a bit, when it was clear I was not going to open them
straight away:
'Aunty Memem? It's nice to share.'

I opened the sweets they'd given me.
And I offered them one (or more than one).
I gave back some of what they had given me.

Psalm 116:12: 'What can I offer the LORD for all he has
done for me?' (NLT).

Hanging on the cross, Jesus thought of others.
He thought of you.
He thought of me.

Philippians 2:3–5: 'in humility value others above yourselves, not looking to your own interests but each of you to
the interests of the others. In your relationships with one
another, have the same mindset as Christ Jesus'.

Lord Jesus
I don't know what to say.
You thought of me?
Beyond the cross,
the pain,
the rejection,
you thought of me?
Before yourself?
May I

in some small way
follow your example.
Amen.

The cry echoes from the cross down through the ages,
'Woman, here is your son'.[1]
It is a humbling cry for
it is a genuine cry.
While enduring the most agonising pain possible,
he thought of others?
'Woman, here is your son'.
So often I put me first.
My feelings.
What I want.
What suits me.
I do want to care.
To be considerate.
And sometimes I am.
But sometimes I'm not.
'Woman, here is your son'.

Oh, Father of all compassion,
help me catch hold of that echo.
Its love,
its genuineness,
and, in doing so, realize that
I can care.
The strength of every echo is
its source.
Your compassion will flow through me

if I permit it.
Help me to listen to your echo.
All it means,
all it stands for.
Enable me to let it resound into my life and days.
May I never let your echo fade.

'Woman, here is your son'.

32

My God, My God, Why Have You Forsaken Me?

God paid a ransom to save you from the empty life you inherited from your ancestors. And it was not paid with mere gold or silver, which lose their value. It was the precious blood of Christ, the sinless, spotless Lamb of God. God chose him as your ransom long before the world began, but now in these last days he has been revealed for your sake.

1 Peter 1:18–20 (NLT)

I was trapped in a tunnel somewhere in Wales. I don't mean literally trapped. I wasn't pinned down or hemmed in. The tunnel was more of a long, low cave. I could, theoretically, be on my feet if I bent over. But, the minute I'd moved beyond the light shining in from the entrance, it was dark. Very dark. And, I discovered, such black darkness left me unable to balance. Later, I'd be told this was due to brain tumours. At the time, I was unaware of the existence of such things in my head. I just knew, stuck in that tunnel, that I couldn't move. Not forwards, not backwards. If I tried, I fell. How stupid. I'd abseiled, canoed, climbed rocks, walked over hills and through streams without a problem. And now, on the final day, I was to be defeated by the dark?

Feeling annoyed with myself, I was convinced I'd soon be able to find my balance in the dark.
I didn't call out to the fading voices and footsteps of the rest of my group.
Because I'd be fine in a minute.

But I wasn't.

Nor the next minute.
By which time my group had well and truly gone.

I'd been left behind.

Then I heard footsteps.
My teacher.
Coming back into the darkness to find me.
Taking my hand,
she led me out.

Exodus 19:4: 'I carried you on eagles' wings and brought you to myself.'

Lord Jesus
Thank you for enduring the cross,
because of the joy you saw before you.[1]
Thank you for considering joy greater than pain.

Even the pain of being separated from your Father.
He turned his face away from you.
A dark I need never know.
I can't even begin to fathom such love.
Amen.

The cry echoes from the cross down through the ages,
'My God, my God, why have you forsaken me?'[2]
It is an amazing cry for
it is a genuine cry.
You had to ask,
you were willing to need to ask,
so I'd never need to.
'My God, my God, why have you forsaken me?'
That's the thing.
You haven't.
And you never will.
Even when I feel you have.
Why do I forget.
Forget to remember you're here.
'My God, my God, why have you forsaken me?'
That's the thing.
You haven't.

Oh, present Father,
help me catch hold of that echo.
its love,
its genuineness,
and, in doing so, realize that
I'm not forsaken.

Jesus was.
You love me that much.
'My God, my God, why have you forsaken me?'
The strength of every echo is
its source.
Reminding me I'm not abandoned.
Ever.
Help me to listen to your echo.
All it means,
all it stands for.
Enable me to let it resound into my life and days.
May I never let your echo fade.

'My God, my God, why have you forsaken me?'
(You haven't.)

33

I Thirst!

For now we see only a reflection as in a mirror; then we shall see face to face. Now I know in part; then I shall know fully, even as I am fully known.

1 Corinthians 13:12

'When we operate, you will lose your hearing,' said the doctor.

Very matter of fact.

And so began a round of seeing various professionals who told me again that I'd lose my hearing,
who advised me on how to manage deafness,
who attempted to teach me sign language.

But none of them could answer the question which loomed largest in my mind.

What's it like?
What's it really like to suddenly inhabit a silent world?

And then I met a doctor who could.

She'd been deafened herself.

What's it like?
She knew.

Hebrews 4:15,16: 'For we do not have a high priest who is unable to feel sympathy for our weaknesses, but we have one who has been tempted in every way, just as we are – yet he did not sin . . .'

What's it like?
He knows.

'. . . Let us then approach God's throne of grace with confidence, so that we may receive mercy and find grace to help us in our time of need.'

Lord Jesus
Thank you that I can never say 'no one understands',
because it's not true.
Even when it feels true,
it's not.
You are right here.
I'm known.
Amen.

The cry echoes from the cross down through the ages,
'I thirst!'[1]
It is an empathetic cry for
it is a genuine cry.
'I thirst.'
He felt need.
Discomfort.
Dehydration.
'I thirst!'
I feel discomfort.
I feel dehydrated.
Worn out.
I need something more than I have.
I, too, thirst.
'I thirst!'

Oh, sharing Father,
help me catch hold of that echo.
Its love,
its genuineness,
and, in doing so, realize that
I'm not misunderstood.
Jesus was.
So I would always be known.
'I thirst!'
The strength of every echo is
its source.
Reminding me I'm recognized.
Always.
By you.

'I thirst!'
Help me to listen to your echo.
All it means,
all it stands for.
Enable me to let it resound into my life and days.
May I never let your echo fade.

'I thirst!'

34

It Is Finished

He does not treat us as our sins deserve or repay us according to our iniquities.
For as high as the heavens are above the earth, so great is his love for those who fear him . . .

Psalm 103:10,11

I was flying a kite with my nephew. Well, attempting to. There was little wind, so the chances of getting the kite airborne were pretty slim, and they were made slimmer by the fact that Josiah was not keen to let go. I'd explained to him that I'd hold the string and he would hold the kite. When I said 'Go!' he was to run as fast as he could with the kite and then, when I shouted, 'Let go!' he was to throw the kite in the air.

Hopefully it would fly.

Except it didn't. Nor did it nosedive. It remained tight in Josiah's hand. He ran as fast as his little legs would carry him but, when it came to the crucial moment of letting go, he just couldn't do it.
'Aunty Memem, why won't it fly?'

Again and again I explained that he needed to let go.

'Why won't it fly?'

Again and again he didn't let go.

Or couldn't let go.

But eventually he could.

He did.
He let go.
And the kite flew.

Proverbs 3:5: 'Trust in the LORD with all your heart and lean not on your own understanding'.

Father God
Why won't it fly?
I know it's because I hold on.
I can't let go.
Or won't.
Or both.
Help me trust.
To release things to you.
And believe that they are gone.
Amen.

The cry echoes from the cross down through the ages, 'It is finished.'[1]

It is a compelling cry for
it is a genuine cry.
'It is finished.'
Dealt with.
Settled.
Complete.
'It is finished.'
Is that really possible?
I know there's a lot in my life still unsettled.
I can't say things are dealt with.
'It is finished.'
But you, who know the end from the beginning, can say it.
Because you dealt with them.
And more.
'It is finished.'

Oh, completing Father,
help me catch hold of that echo.
Its love,
its genuineness,
and, in doing so, realize that
victory is possible.
I can let go.
'It is finished.'
The strength of every echo is
its source.
Reminding me of possibilities.
Of strength.
In you.
'It is finished.'

Help me to listen to your echo.
All it means,
all it stands for.
Enable me to let it resound into my life and days.
May I never let your echo fade.

'It is finished.'

35

Into Your Hands I Commit My Spirit

'For I know the plans I have for you,' says the LORD. 'They are plans for good and not for disaster, to give you a future and a hope.'
Jeremiah 29:11 (NLT)

One February, my mum said to me, 'Keep the last weekend in May free.'

I asked why?

She answered, 'It's a surprise.'

Now, I'm someone who likes surprises I know about!

Or so I thought.

Which is why I spent the next few weeks wondering what the surprise could be and worrying that I might not like it.

Then suddenly, in a eureka moment, I stopped worrying.

And I stopped wondering.

I remembered what I'd always known but hadn't applied to the unknown:

my parents loved me.

They wouldn't deliberately give me a surprise I wouldn't like.

More importantly, even if it did turn out to be a bad surprise, it wouldn't be terrible.

It would be good in its own way.
Because my parents, who loved me, would be with me.
So, better late than never, I let go of needing to be in control of my own surprise.
I stopped wondering and worrying.
It was enough that someone who loved me knew.

1 Corinthians 2:9: 'No eye has seen, no ear has heard, and no mind has imagined what God has prepared for those who love him' (NLT).

Father God
You know tomorrow.
You know all my tomorrows.
It's better that you know
and I don't.
I know that really.
But sometimes I find it hard.
Help me to trust you.
To let go of needing to know.
To let your knowing be enough.
Amen.

The cry echoes from the cross down through the ages,
'Into your hands I commit my spirit.'[1]
It is a confident cry for
it is a genuine cry.
'Into your hands I commit my spirit.'
He trusted his Father.
And he proved it.

By giving everything.
Everything he was,
Jesus gave.
Wholeheartedly.
'Into your hands I commit my spirit.'
I need that trust,
that conviction,
that courage.
'Into your hands I commit my spirit.'
Letting go of my claim on me?
My control on my life?
I want to.
Wholeheartedly.
But it's hard.
And yet, the echo is there.
Resounding.

Oh, Father of all fearlessness,
help me catch hold of that echo.
It's love,
its genuineness,
And, in doing so, realize that
release is attainable.
I can let go of control.
And hand it to you.
'Into your hands I commit my spirit.'
The strength of every echo is
its source.
The origin of freedom is
in you.

'Into your hands I commit my spirit.'
Help me to listen to your echo.
All it means,
all it stands for.
Enable me to let it resound into my life and days.
May I never let your echo fade.

'Into your hands I commit my spirit.'

Part 6

Add to Faith

2 Peter 1:3: 'His divine power has given us everything we need for a godly life through our knowledge of him who called us by his own glory and goodness.'

Power.
'The ability to do something'.[1]
We have a powerful God.
He can create the world, speak from a burning bush, calm the storm.
We know he is able.
He is powerful.
But maybe we sometimes forget how far-reaching his power is.
It reaches all the way to us.
To me.
To you.

Romans 12:2: 'Don't copy the behavior and customs of this world, but let God transform you into a new person by changing the way you think' (NLT).

God at work.
In you.
His power.
In you.
You have 'the ability to do something'.
In this case, live a godly life.

2 Peter 1:5–7: 'For this very reason, make every effort to add to your faith goodness; and to goodness, knowledge; and to knowledge, self-control; and to self-control, perseverance; and to perseverance, godliness; and to godliness, mutual affection; and to mutual affection, love.'

36

Goodness

Therefore, as God's chosen people, holy and dearly loved, clothe yourselves with compassion, kindness, humility, gentleness and patience. Bear with each other and forgive one another if any of you has a grievance against someone. Forgive as the Lord forgave you.

Colossians 3:12,13

Little feet padded up the stairs and a head popped around the corner of the room where I was getting ready.

I was on holiday with friends and my 6-year-old god-daughter had wandered into my villa, wondering where I was. She was all ready to go out for dinner and had come to find me.

I was nearly ready and was just straightening my hair. Amaya was fascinated. Dinner forgotten, she asked, 'Can you do my hair like that?' There was no time then, but I told her I would the following evening.

Sure enough, the next evening, little feet padded up the stairs.

'Is it time?' She'd been asking on and off all day and, finally, it was time.

She sat down at the dressing table and stayed like a statue while I straightened her curly hair. When I'd finished, I suggested she take a look in the mirror. Standing up, she looked at her reflection, turning her head back and forth. Then she turned to me.

'Look! I've got your hair.'

Her hair did look very similar to mine.

But she didn't say, 'Our hair looks the same.'

'I've got your hair.'

I've got part of you.

John 14:20,21: 'I am in my Father, and you are in me, and I am in you. Whoever has my commands and keeps them is the one who loves me.'

With Jesus in us, we can do and be who he wants us to be. Because we are a part of him.
So close.
I can do the things I think impossible,
I can be the person I long to be
because I've got you.

Lord Jesus
Look! You are in me.
Help me to live like you.
I am in you.
Help me to become like you.
You in me.
Me in you.
Apart from you, I can do nothing.
Amen.

Today, I choose goodness.
Because goodness has been chosen for me,
goodness is possible.
The ability to respond with grace has been
placed within me.
I must believe that.
To doubt a truth is to believe a lie.
But the lie is more believable than the truth.
How can goodness be a part of who I'm created
to be?
I lose my temper.
I get frustrated.
I lash out.
People annoy me.
I annoy me.
And yet, goodness is a part of me now.
It's in there somewhere.
Always accessible.
God has promised.

I can be the person he made me to be.
Reflecting the goodness of my creator.
Pushing aside my doubts to reveal his truth.
Certain that
goodness is possible.
God has promised.
Because goodness has been chosen for me
today
I choose goodness.

37

Knowledge

I pray that you, being rooted and established in love, may have power, together with all the Lord's holy people, to grasp how wide and long and high and deep is the love of Christ, and to know this love that surpasses knowledge – that you may be filled to the measure of all the fullness of God.

Ephesians 3:17–19

We were playing with dolls. Or building blocks. I can't remember which, and it doesn't matter. Suddenly, apropos of nothing, Charis looked up at me and said, 'You love me, don't you?' And then she turned her attention back to the toys.

'You love me, don't you?'

Matter of fact.
A rhetorical question.
She knew the answer would never be 'no',
and she was right.

She knew because I have loved her since the day she was born. And, since the day she was born, I have told her so.

'I love you' as I pushed her on a swing. 'I love you' as I tickled her and made her giggle. 'I love you' as I tucked her in and kissed her goodnight.

When she was 3, my goddaughter asked me, with total security in the answer, 'You love me, don't you?'

'Yes, sweetie-pie, I do.'

1 John 3:1: 'See how very much our Father loves us, for he calls us his children, and that is what we are!' (NLT).

'*Abba*,
you love me, don't you?'

Yes, my child; I do.

Father God
Those times when I doubt,
when I feel unlovable
by anyone,
even you,
help me have the courage to lift my eyes up.
To stop saying 'But what about . . .'
And instead whisper,
'You love me, don't you?'
Believing your *yes*.
Amen.

Today, I choose knowledge.

Because knowledge has been chosen for me,
knowledge is possible.
The ability to know has been
placed within me.
I must believe that.
To doubt a truth is to believe a lie.
But the lie is more believable than the truth.
How can knowing be a part of who I'm created
to be?
That in itself is beyond my understanding.
I grapple with my unknowing.
What is it I should know?
God loves me.
I know.
I forget to know.
And yet, knowledge is a part of me now.
It's in there somewhere.
Always accessible.
God has promised.
I can know that I am loved.
Reflecting the knowledge of my creator.
Pushing aside my doubts to reveal his truth.
Certain that
knowledge is possible.
God has promised.
Because knowledge has been chosen for me
today
I choose knowledge.

38

Self-control

. . . take captive every thought to make it obedient to Christ.
2 Corinthians 10:5

I could see he was tempted. The silver-wrapped chocolate coin in his hand did look tasty. It was probably as good as the one he'd just eaten. But I'd said he could take one, not two. 'Josiah,' I said, 'If you don't put that sweet back, we won't go to the park.'

Sweet,
park,
sweet,
park.

He began to unwrap the chocolate.
'Think about it,' I said.
Josiah loves going to the park.
Swings, running, sticks to play with . . .

'Think about it.'

Sweet,

park,
sweet,
park.

He put the sweet back.
And we went to the park.
Together.

Sometimes we forget that our actions have consequences.
Consequences which may cause us to miss out.
And to grow apart from God.

Psalm 119:59: 'I have considered my ways and have turned
my steps to your statutes.'

Father God
I'm asking for your help.
I don't find that easy to do
but here I am.
Asking.
Please help me to think before I speak.
Consider before I act.
I don't want to miss out
on anything
from you.
Amen.

Today, I choose self-control.
Because self-control has been chosen for me,
self-control is possible.

The ability to choose my attitude has been
placed within me.
I must believe that.
To doubt a truth is to believe a lie.
But the lie is more believable than the truth.
How can self-control be a part of who I'm created
to be?
So often my behaviour is the boss
I helplessly follow.
I have no choice and my impotence overwhelms me.
I get angry with the behaviour I see
in me.
I do
what I don't want to do.
I say things.
They can't be unsaid.
And yet, self-control is a part of me now.
It's in there somewhere.
Always accessible.
God has promised.
I can be the person he made me to be.
In him.
Pushing aside my doubts to reveal his truth.
Certain that
self-control is possible.
God has promised.
Because self-control has been chosen for me
today
I choose self-control.

39

Perseverance

But encourage one another daily, as long as it is called 'Today', so that none of you may be hardened by sin's deceitfulness.

Hebrews 3:13

When I was at school, I was part of the cross-country team. Every Saturday during winter, I would go to the race location, and I would run. Sometimes it was a beautiful day, cold and frosty and perfect for running. Sometimes it was raining. Sometimes it was muddy. Sometimes uphill. Downhill. Through puddles. Across paths.

But there was something there in every race: the home straight.

It always seemed to be around a corner, so I didn't see it until near the end of the race, when I was tired. Sometimes even thinking of giving up. And then the home straight came into view. I was nearly there. Yet not as nearly as I thought. It looked as though I still had miles to run before I reached the tunnel; a rather grand name for two pieces of rope hung horizontally beside each other.

Every week, rain or shine, my dad was there.
Standing by the home straight.
Cheering me on.
'Come on, Em! You can do it! Nearly there!'

And do you know what?
He was right.
Every time.

Philippians 4:13: 'For I can do everything through Christ,
who gives me strength' (NLT).

Father God
Thank you that you cheer me on.
I'm close to giving up, yet
somehow
your support helps me take a step.
And another.
And I keep going.
Because you cheer me on.
Thank you for supporting me.
Amen.

Today, I choose perseverance.
Because perseverance has been chosen for me,
perseverance is possible.
The ability to keep going has been
placed within me.
I must believe that.
To doubt a truth is to believe a lie.

But the lie is more believable than the truth.
How can perseverance be a part of who I'm created
to be?
Sometimes I can't get going, never mind
keep going.
I'm tired.
Tired of doing which leads to nothing.
Tired of forcing one foot in front of the other.
Day after identical day.
Nothing changes.
I'm weary of it.
And yet, perseverance is a part of me now.
It's in there somewhere.
Always accessible.
God has promised.
I can be the person he made me to be.
Finding joy as I hold on to his way.
Pushing aside my doubts to reveal his truth.
Certain that
perseverance is possible.
God has promised.
Because perseverance has been chosen for me
today
I choose perseverance.

40

Godliness

You have searched me, Lord, and you know me.

Psalm 139:1

He collapsed on the finishing line. Checking his stopwatch, he dragged himself to his feet and set off again, running around the athletics track as fast as he could. He'd been running all afternoon. He must have checked his watch dozens of times. There was a bit of a pattern. Start the clock, sprint around the track, stop the clock. Each time, the clock showed he was a few seconds off his target. 'Must run faster,' he muttered to himself as he set off again. He wanted to make the national team. It had become his life's focus. He was so nearly there, but not quite.

A man stood at a distance, watching. Round and round and round. The athlete was going to do himself an injury. The man walked over to the finishing line. The runner had collapsed on it, breathing hard, a look of defeat on his face as he realized that once again, he had narrowly missed his target. Maybe he couldn't do it after all. He was just kidding himself.

Looking up, he saw his coach. Crouching down beside the exhausted figure, the coach reached for the stopwatch. The athlete tried to hide the watch, clenching it in his fist. He knew he'd failed. His coach would be so disappointed in him.

'I can't do it,' he whispered.

Gently prising the stopwatch from his hand, his coach looked at the time. It was well within the qualifying range. The coach switched the watch off.

'You already have.'

So often, we try and try to be who God wants us to be, convinced we are failing. Every time. Yet, like the athlete, we get the benchmark wrong. We aim for the wrong thing. We think we need to do things we don't need to do.

And so, in our failing, we miss the fact that we haven't failed at all.

2 Peter 1:3: 'His divine power has given us everything we need for a godly life through our knowledge of him who called us'.

Matthew 19:26: 'Jesus looked at them intently and said, 'Humanly speaking, it is impossible. But with God everything is possible' (NLT).

God never asks the impossible.
He knows us, so much better than we know ourselves.
With God
'impossible'
is nothing.
He takes away our self-imposed stopwatch.

'I can't do it.'

'You already have.'

Father God
I try and try, but
I can't do it.
I fail, so often.
Yet, maybe I don't.
Help me to know you more.
To know what you ask.
And what you don't.
So I can freely live.
Amen.

Today, I choose godliness.
Because godliness has been chosen for me,
godliness is possible.
The ability to live as God wants has been
placed within me.
I must believe that.
To doubt a truth is to believe a lie.
But the lie is more believable than the truth.

How can godliness be a part of who I'm created
to be?
God is so far above me
in every sense.
How can I begin to reach for what he wants,
let alone comprehend it?
I don't think I can.
And yet, godliness is a part of me now.
It's in there somewhere.
Always accessible.
God has promised.
I can be the person he made me to be.
Knowing him more as I learn more of him.
Pushing aside my doubts to reveal his truth.
Certain that
godliness is possible.
God has promised.
Because godliness has been chosen for me
today
I choose godliness.

41

Mutual Affection

For God so loved the world that he gave his one and only Son,
that whoever believes in him shall not perish but have eternal life.
John 3:16

A friend invited me to a Christmas craft evening at her church. When we got there, everyone was given a plain wooden plaque which was shaped to make the word 'love'. Along with the plaques, there were identical bags of stickers with which to decorate them. We picked up our wooden plaques, which all looked the same, and opened our bags of stickers, which all looked the same, and began sticking, chatting as we did. At the end, I looked at my plaque. To my surprise, it wasn't bad. I am not good with crafts but this time it seemed I'd done a reasonable job. I looked around the table at the other plaques. They all looked good, too.

But, as I looked, I realized that none of our plaques looked the same.

The word was the same.
The stickers were the same.

But we'd all placed our stickers differently.

Love looked different for everyone.
And everyone had love.
Including me.

Lamentations 3:22,23: 'The faithful love of the LORD never ends! His mercies never cease. Great is his faithfulness; his mercies begin afresh each morning' (NLT).

Father God
Thank you that, in you,
through you,
everyone has love.
Everyone in the whole world.
Including me.
Amen.

Today, I choose mutual affection.
Because mutual affection has been chosen for me,
mutual affection is possible.
The ability to honour and be esteemed has been placed within me.
I must believe that.
To doubt a truth is to believe a lie.
But the lie is more believable than the truth.
How can mutual affection be a part of who I'm created to be?
I esteem.
I'm not esteemed.

People tell me I am.
They tell me my worth
but I struggle to believe it.
Sometimes I don't believe it.
I try but
I can't.
Giving is easier than receiving.
And yet, mutual affection is a part of me now.
It's in there somewhere.
Always accessible.
God has promised.
I can be the person he made me to be.
Allowing myself to be valued.
Esteemed.
Pushing aside my doubts to reveal his truth.
Certain that
mutual affection is possible.
God has promised.
Because mutual affection has been chosen for me
today
I choose mutual affection.

42

Love

Blessed are the peacemakers, for they will be called children of God.

Matthew 5:9

My niece spontaneously jumped up and wrapped her little arms tight around my neck. 'I love you,' she whispered in my ear.

So I'm told, anyway.

I am deaf. I didn't hear her.

Someone else did and told me what she'd said.
She'd told me she loved me, and I'd missed it.

I felt overwhelmingly sad.
I wished I'd heard her.

Part of me was also a bit sceptical.
Had she really said that?
She'd never said it before.

As she grew older, she learned that I can't hear.
She still wraps her arms around my neck.
But now, before she tells me she loves me,
she pulls back
so I can read her lips.

1 John 4:7: 'Dear friends, let us love one another, for love
comes from God.'

Father God
People are all different.
Help me to remember that's OK.
Different is good.
It's how you made us.
It's how you love us.
Help us, help me, to love others.
Amen.

Today, I choose love.
Because love has been chosen for me,
love is possible.
Compassion has been
placed within me.
I must believe that.
To doubt a truth is to believe a lie.
But the lie is more believable than the truth.
How can love be a part of who I'm created
to be?
Wanting the best, not the easiest,
all the time.

Believing the best, not the meanest,
all the time.
Not expecting too much,
all the time.
Allowing people to be themselves,
all the time.
And yet, love is a part of me now.
It's in there somewhere.
Always accessible.
God has promised.
I can be the person he made me to be.
Loving others.
And myself.
Pushing aside my doubts to reveal his truth.
Certain that
love is possible.
God has promised.
Because love has been chosen for me
today
I choose love.

Part 7

Revelation Churches

In this final section, we look at the letters to the seven churches in the book of Revelation, chapters 2 and 3: Ephesus, Smyrna, Pergamum, Thyatira, Sardis, Philadelphia and Laodicea.

Perhaps there's something of each one in all of us.

Ephesians 5:25–27:

'Christ loved the church and gave himself up for her to make her holy, cleansing her by the washing with water through the word, and to present her to himself as a radiant church, without stain or wrinkle or any other blemish, but holy and blameless.'

The anaesthetic started to wear off and I came round.

Usually, I'm told, when I come round from an anaesthetic, I start chattering away, nineteen to the dozen. I never remember it though.

This time was different. I remember with absolute clarity the time I came round from a lengthy and complicated operation on my spine.

Lying flat on the bed, with my head raised slightly by pillows, I opened my eyes. I took in the fact that I was in transit from the recovery room to a ward. I was beside a nurses' station and people were discussing where they should put me.

I noticed the pale green thin hospital blanket covering me. I saw my parents' faces above me, Mum first and Dad right behind her. I looked again at the blanket, my legs stretched underneath it.

I shifted my legs.
The blanket didn't move.

I tried again.
The blanket didn't move.

I turned to my mum, panic-stricken:
'I can't move my legs.'

She leaned over the raised bedside between us and took my hand.
'I know you can't, Em, but it will come.'

Long weeks later, it came.
My legs moved.

And, eventually, I stood.

1 Corinthians 13:12: 'Now we see things imperfectly, like puzzling reflections in a mirror, but then we will see everything with perfect clarity. All that I know now is partial and incomplete, but then I will know everything completely, just as God now knows me completely' (NLT).

I know you can't, but it will come . . .

Within the seven churches, we meet people like us.
People for whom life is not always easy.
People who struggle.
People who are trying to balance work life and spiritual life in a world which laughs at them and puts them down.
People who swim against the tide to hold on to their faith.
People who look at their own lives and feel worthless.
People who find every day difficult.
People who feel they can't keep going.
People who, despite everything, cling on to hope.
People who hold on to heaven, even when life's hard.
People who believe that better things lie ahead.

I know you can't, but it will come . . .

43

Ephesus

*Love the L*ORD *your God with all your heart and with all your soul and with all your strength.*

Deuteronomy 6:5

Dear Child

I'm writing to your inner Ephesus, to let it – and you – know that I know.

I know all you do. Every single thing. When you keep going; I know. When you bite back a sharp retort; I know. When you do the right thing even when it's hard; I know. When you are exhausted but never think of giving up following me; I know. When you stand up for what is right; I know.

I know you.

So I also know that you have forgotten to love me as you did.

Remember back at the beginning, when you loved me with all your heart?
You did things because you love me.

Now you do things because . . .
Why do you do them?

You'll say it's for me.
I know.
And it's true.

But is so much doing squashing some of the love from the
doing?

We don't seem to spend much time together any more,
just being you and me.
Do you think that could change?
I'd like it to.

And even when you're on the go,
be with me in your heart.
I miss you.

I know life is not always easy.
I know your life and
I know what it will be.

One day, my little Ephesus,
my faithful one,
my child,
victory for you will look like time to stop
and eat
from the tree of life
in the paradise of God.

No more striving.

I hold the seven stars in my right hand.
I walk among seven golden lampstands.

I'm with you.
And, at the same time, I'm in heaven.
Waiting for you.

Hold fast.
I know you.
And I'm coming for you soon . . .

Jesus

Psalm 95:6: 'Come, let us bow down in worship, let us kneel before the Lord our Maker'.

Lord Jesus
I am busy.
I know I am.
Am I so busy doing things,
I forget why I am doing them?
I think I am.
Do I lose sight of you?
I think I do.
Help me to love you with my whole heart.
Amen.

44

Smyrna

*God will meet all your needs according to the riches of his glory
in Christ Jesus.*

Philippians 4:19

Dear Child

I'm writing to your inner Smyrna, to let it – and you – know
that I know.

I know how tough life is. How difficult. How painful.
How hard.
How other people lie about you and torture you and put
you down.

I also know that more troubles lie ahead.
I'm not telling you that to make you scared.
I'm telling you because I want to say to you
whisper to you
lock into your heart
'Don't be afraid.'

I know.

I know that what you don't have makes you feel insufficient.
But I know that you are rich.

Yes, my child, you are.
You are rich in what matters.
Matters not to the world,
but to me.

Stay faithful to your wealth.
You are not inadequate.

I know your life and
I know what it will be.

One day, my little Smyrna,
my priceless one,
my child,
victory for you will look like
a laurel crown.

Life in all its fullness.
Forever.
No more hurting.

I am the First and the Last.
I died and came back to life.

I'm here.
And, at the same time, I'm in heaven.
Waiting for you.

Be brave.
I know you.
And I'm coming for you soon . . .

Jesus

2 Corinthians 4:18: 'We fix our eyes not on what is seen, but on what is unseen, since what is seen is temporary, but what is unseen is eternal.'

Lord Jesus
I'm not very brave.
Life overwhelms me.
Other people overwhelm me.
Yet you whisper to me,
'Don't be afraid.'
Help me to listen.
Amen.

45

Pergamum

For where your treasure is, there your heart will be also.

Luke 12:34

Dear Child

I'm writing to your inner Pergamum, to let it – and you – know that I know.

I know you're swimming against the tide so often.
Surrounded by people who don't follow me.
Who mock you for following me.
Who think you're weak.
Brainwashed.

I know it's hard.
Yet nothing makes you deny your faith.

Yes, my child; I know that, too.
Hold on to my knowing.

But could you also let go?

Let go of the things you allow in your life
that shouldn't be there?
The things that draw you away from following me
wholeheartedly?

I know them, too.
They worm their way in.
Don't let them do that.

I know it's hard to stop them.
But do it in my name.

I know your life and
I know what it will be.

One day, my little Pergamum,
my resilient one,
my child,
victory for you will look like
the purity of hidden manna,
given to you.

Victory will look like a white stone,
inscribed with a new name.
A name known only to you
and me.
No more separation.

I have the double-edged sword.

I see good and bad.

I'm here.
And, at the same time, I'm in heaven.
Waiting for you.

Stay true.
I know you.
And I'm coming for you soon . . .

Jesus

1 Thessalonians 5:21: 'Test everything that is said. Hold on to what is good' (NLT).

Lord Jesus
Help me to keep following you.
Sometimes it is hard,
but I never want my life to deny you.
Ever.
May I put you first.
Always.
And honour you in all I do.
Amen.

46

Thyatira

I am the vine; you are the branches. If you remain in me and I in you, you will bear much fruit; apart from me you can do nothing.

John 15:5

Dear Child

I'm writing to your inner Thyatira, to let it – and you – know that I know.

I know all you do.
Every day.
I know you do it with such love and faithfulness.

And I know you are growing.
It delights me to see that you are now able to do more and different things.
Don't stop growing and learning.
Ever.

But that part of you,
that little part,
which persuades you things are OK when they're not?

That little voice you have inside
which says, 'This won't affect my faithfulness.'
That doesn't delight me.

Because those things will affect how close you and I can be.
And I don't want things to get in the way of us.
Do you?

Hold tight to the truly good things.

I know your life and
I know what it will be.

One day, my little Thyatira,
my maturing one,
my child,
victory for you will look like
the morning star.

I will give you the morning star.
And I will give you authority.
No more compromise.

I am the Son of God.
My eyes blaze like fire,
my feet shine like bronze.
No room for impurity.

I'm here.
And, at the same time, I'm in heaven.

Waiting for you.

Don't be defiled.
I know you.
And I'm coming for you soon . . .

Jesus

Colossians 1:10: 'live a life worthy of the Lord and please him in every way: bearing fruit in every good work, growing in the knowledge of God'.

Lord Jesus
Thank you for growing me in you.
For moving me on.
For enlarging my faith.
But I know there are things in the way.
Things in my life which won't help me grow.
Or which stop me growing as I could.
They need to go.
I know.
Help me to be discerning.
I want to live a life set apart for you.
Amen.

47

Sardis

*The thief comes only to steal and kill and destroy; I have come
that they may have life, and have it to the full.*

John 10:10

Dear Child

I'm writing to your inner Sardis, to let it – and you – know
that I know.

I know all you do.

I know people look at you and see a vibrant, capable, strong
person.
But, because I know you, I see beyond your mask.
I see you.

Behind the mask of coping
is someone pretending to live.
Someone fading.

Don't become lost.
You're still in there.

Remember all you have.
Hold on to it.

Live!

I know you.
So I know there's a little bit of you that is holding on already.
That's good.
Reach to grasp more.

I know your life and
I know what it will be.

One day, my little Sardis,
my unmasked one,
my child,
victory for you will look like
honesty.

No disguise.
I will dress you in white.
Dazzling white.

Your name, my child, will be in the book of life.
Real life.
No pretence.
And I will proclaim your name
to my Father.

I hold the sevenfold Spirit of God.

I hold the seven stars.

I also hold you.

I'm here.
And, at the same time, I'm in heaven.
Waiting for you.

Don't be hidden.
I know you.
And I'm coming for you soon . . .

Jesus

Isaiah 49:16: 'See, I have engraved you on the palms of my hands'.

Lord Jesus
Why am I surprised you see through my mask of coping?
Of course you see through it.
You know me better than I know myself.
Help me to be real,
to accept me as I am.
Just as you accept me.
Please hold on to me.
Don't let me go.
Amen.

48

Philadelphia

Strengthen the feeble hands, steady the knees that give way; say to those with fearful hearts, 'Be strong, do not fear; your God will come'.

Isaiah 35:3,4

Dear Child

I'm writing to your inner Philadelphia, to let it – and you – know that I know.

I know you feel weak.
Your strength almost gone.

Yet you don't deny me.
You stay true.

Look up ahead, little one.
There's an open door that no one can shut.
No one.
Not even those liars.
The ones who tell you they know best,
who overpower and drown you out.

They don't know.
But one day they will.
One day they will acknowledge that
I love you.

Look up.

I know your life and
I know what it will be.

One day, my little Philadelphia,
my courageous one,
my child,
victory for you will look like
strength.

Standing tall.
A mighty pillar in the temple of my God.
Forever.

I will write on the pillar that is you.
I will write the name of my God.
The name of his city.
And I will write my new name.

You will belong.
And everyone will know.

I am holy and true.

Doors I open, no one can shut.
I hold the key.

I also hold you.

I'm here.
And, at the same time, I'm in heaven.
Waiting for you.

Don't despair.
I know you.
And I'm coming for you soon . . .

Jesus

Psalm 24:9: 'Lift up your heads, you gates; lift them up, you ancient doors, that the King of glory may come in.'

Lord Jesus
My strength has gone.
To be honest, I can't even remember what strength feels like.
I cling on, but I feel
so weak.
And useless.
No one wants to know me.
Except you.
You give me new strength for now and
courage for tomorrow.
Thank you.
Amen.

49

Laodicea

A person is a fool to store up earthly wealth but not have a rich relationship with God.

Luke 12:21 (NLT)

Dear Child

I'm writing to your inner Laodicea, to let it – and you – know that I know.

I know what you do.
I know what you say.
'I'm rich, I'm sorted, I don't need a thing.'

I know.

I also know, my child, that you're wrong.
You're not rich.
Not in what matters.
You're not.
But you can be.

Come to me.
I'll give you wealth and beauty beyond compare.
I'll clothe you in white.
Regal white.

I know you are lukewarm,
undecided,
swaying with the wind,
not sure who to follow,
lurching this way and that.
You need to stop.
Now.

I'm only telling you this because I love you so much.
I want the best for you.
I'm knocking at the door.
The handle is on your side.
It's up to you to open it
and let me in.

I promise I'll come.
And I'll sit down with you.
Whatever it is like behind that door,
I'll stay.

I know your life and
I know what it will be.

One day, my little Laodicea,
my floundering one,

my child,
because you opened the door,
victory for you will look like
nobility.
Rooted.
Unwavering.

Sitting with me on my throne.
As I sat,
victorious,
with my Father
on his throne.

I am faithful and true.
I am the Amen.
The 'Let it be'.
The ruler of God's creation.
Including you.

Let it be.

I'm here.
And, at the same time, I'm in heaven.
Waiting for you.

Believe.
I know you.
And I'm coming for you soon . . .

Jesus

Matthew 13:45,46: 'The Kingdom of Heaven is like a merchant on the lookout for choice pearls. When he discovered a pearl of great value, he sold everything he owned and bought it!' (NLT).

Lord Jesus
Self-sufficient.
That would be a good way to describe me.
I'm not good at relying on anything.
Or anyone.
But I can rely on you, can't I?
Help me to trust you.
To believe with all my heart that you are
the only way.
And to live that belief.
God-sufficient.
Amen.

Revelation 21:1–4,22,23: 'Then I saw a new heaven and a new earth, for the old heaven and the old earth had disappeared. And the sea was also gone. And I saw the holy city, the new Jerusalem, coming down from God out of heaven like a bride beautifully dressed for her husband.

'I heard a loud shout from the throne, saying, "Look, God's home is now among his people! He will live with them, and they will be his people. God himself will be with them. He will wipe every tear from their eyes, and there will be no more death or sorrow or crying or pain. All these things are gone forever."'

'I saw no temple in the city, for the Lord God Almighty and the Lamb are its temple. And the city has no need of sun or moon, for the glory of God illuminates the city, and the Lamb is its light' (NLT).

Notes

Preface

[1] Regarding my ability to hear in some of the anecdotes but not in others: I lost my hearing at the age of 21.

29 Father, Forgive

[1] Luke 23:34.

30 Today You Will Be with Me in Paradise

[1] Luke 23:43.

31 Woman, Here Is Your Son

[1] John 19:26.

32 My God, My God, Why Have You Forsaken Me?

1 See Hebrews 12:2.
2 Psalm 22:1.

33 I Thirst!

1 John 19:28, NKJV.

34 It Is Finished

1 John 19:30.

35 Into Your Hands I Commit My Spirit

1 Luke 23:46.

Part 6 Add to Faith

1 https://uk.search.yahoo.com/search?fr=mcafee&type=
   D211GB642G0&p=power+definition (accessed 14.5.18).

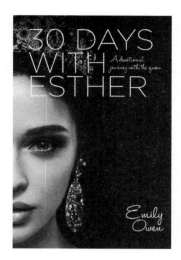

30 Days with Esther

*A devotional journey with
the queen*

Emily Owen

By imagining the diaries of familiar figures from the Bible, Emily Owen draws us into their lives. She then leads us in contemplation, often taking a surprising direction. Gently challenging, each day draws us closer to God.

What must it have been like to be Esther, transformed from an orphaned Jew in exile to Queen of Persia? This thirty-day devotional look at 'Esther's diary' has thought-provoking points, prayers and questions to help explore this much-loved story in a new way.

978-1-78078-448-9
978-1-78078-450-2 (e-book)

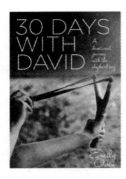

30 Days with David
A devotional journey with the shepherd boy
Emily Owen

978-1-78078-449-6
978-1-78078-451-9 (e-book)

30 Days with John
A devotional journey with the disciple
Emily Owen

978-1-86024-936-5
978-1-78078-257-7 (e-book)

30 Days with Mary
A devotional journey with the mother of Jesus
Emily Owen

978-1-86024-935-8
978-1-78078-255-3 (e-book)

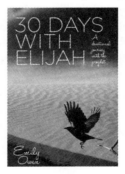

30 Days with Elijah
A devotional journey with the prophet
Emily Owen

978-1-86024-937-2
978-1-78078-256-0 (e-book)

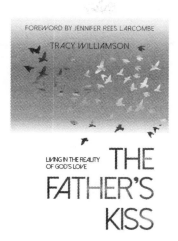

The Father's Kiss

*Living in the reality of
God's Love*

Tracy Williamson

Tracy Williamson honestly shares the insights and lessons she has learned on her own journey to freedom. With a unique mix of practical teaching, personal stories, poems, prophecies and questions for reflection, this is a life-changing resource for all who carry the wounds of rejection.

978-1-78078-988-0
978-1-78078-989-7 (e-book)

God Conversations

*Stories of how God speaks and
what happens when we listen*

Tania Harris

Stories of God talking to his people abound throughout the Bible, but we usually only get the highlights. We read: 'God said "Go to Egypt,"' and then, 'Mary and Joseph left for Egypt.' We're not told how God spoke, how they knew it was him, or how they decided to act on what they'd heard.

In *God Conversations*, international speaker and pastor Tania Harris shares insights from her own story of learning to hear God's voice. You'll get to eavesdrop on some contemporary conversations with God in the light of his communication with the ancients. Part memoir, part teaching, this unique and creative collection will help you to recognize God's voice when he speaks and what happens when you do.

978-1-78078-188-4
978-1-78078-189-1 (e-book)

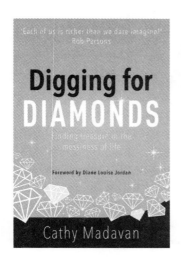

Digging for Diamonds

*Finding treasure in the
messiness of life*

Cathy Madavan

What is hidden always shapes what we can see. In this book, Cathy Madavan encourages us to dig deeper and discover more of the life-transforming treasures of our identity, strength, character and purpose that God has already placed within us – right where we are.

Cathy explores twelve key facets which point the reader to a deeper understanding of their unique, God-given raw material and how God wants to transform them to live a valuable, purposeful life that will also unearth precious potential in others.

978-1-78078-131-0
978-1-78078-247-8 (e-book)

Authentic

We trust you enjoyed reading this book
from Authentic. If you want to be
informed of any new titles from this author
and other releases you can sign up to the
Authentic newsletter by scanning below:

Online:
authenticmedia.co.uk

Follow us: